The name of Helen Keller [is known all over the] world. The achievements of Helen Keller, against su[p]posedly insurmountable odds, have won the admiration and profound respect of everyone who knows her story.

Here is that story—the story of a little girl who once lived in a dark and silent prison. It was lonely in there, and frightening, but try as she would, the little girl could not get out. No sounds of children laughing or of birds singing ever reached her. She never saw the blue sky nor even a friendly smiling face. It is no wonder that the little girl, who was not yet seven, often fell into a rage because she felt so helpless and bewildered.

Then, finally, someone unlocked the door of the prison, and at last Helen was able to walk out into the world. That someone was Anne Sullivan Macy, Helen's beloved "Teacher," and this is Annie Sullivan's story too.

In time, as a result of Helen's eagerness to learn and Teacher's selfless devotion, Helen was ready for college. But no one would believe that a girl who could neither see nor hear could possibly stay the course. Helen wrote to Radcliffe College that "a true soldier does not acknowledge defeat before the battle." And in June, 1904, Helen Keller graduated from Radcliffe "cum laude."

Young readers everywhere will be thrilled by this tender and inspiring story of how courage and determination transformed a pitiful child, left blind, deaf and dumb, into the wise and lovely person admired today the whole world over.

This TEMPO BOOKS *edition contains the complete text of the original hard-cover edition, published by Grosset & Dunlap, Inc., at $1.95*

You will find the same absorbing reading and high quality in other TEMPO BOOKS. Look for them wherever books are sold. If your dealer does not have the TEMPO BOOKS you want, you may order them by mail, enclosing the list price plus 10¢ a copy to cover mailing. A complete list of titles is available free from TEMPO BOOKS, Grosset & Dunlap, Inc., 51 Madison Avenue, New York, New York 10010; some of the books you will enjoy are listed in the back of this book.

THE STORY OF
HELEN KELLER

The Story of

HELEN KELLER

BY LORENA A. HICKOK

ENID LAMONTE MEADOWCROFT
Supervising Editor

*Presented to
Lennis Vaugn Troyer
in 1965
By Grandma Troyer*

TEMPO BOOKS

GROSSET & DUNLAP

NEW YORK

LIBRARY OF CONGRESS CATALOG CARD NO.: 58-9836

TEMPO BOOKS EDITION, 1964

THIS BOOK IS ALSO AVAILABLE IN A HARD-COVER
EDITION AND IN LIBRARY BINDING

FIRST PRINTING, FEBRUARY 1964
SECOND PRINTING, SEPTEMBER 1964

PRINTED IN THE UNITED STATES OF AMERICA

In Grateful Memory of
TEACHER
Who led a little girl out of the dark
And gave to the world . . .
HELEN KELLER

loved than she had been. Everybody noticed it.
she did but have . . . many tantrums. And when
she did have one it . . . not last very long.

Contents

THE STORY OF
HELEN KELLER

1.

Little Girl in the Dark

IT WAS a warm summer evening in the sleepy little town of Tuscumbia, Alabama. A light breeze rustled through the ivy leaves and brought the fragrance of roses into the living room of the vine-covered Keller house.

Captain Arthur Keller laid down his newspaper and peered thoughtfully over his glasses at his six-year-old daughter Helen, curled up in a chair with a big, shapeless rag doll.

"Her mind — whatever mind she has — is locked up in a prison cell," he said sadly. "It can't get out, and nobody can open the door to reach it. For the key is lost and nobody can find it."

Helen's mother looked up from her sewing. Tears filled her eyes.

But the child's aunt spoke up spiritedly in her defense.

"I tell you, Arthur," she said, "Helen's got more sense than all the rest of the Kellers put together."

Captain Keller shook his head and picked up his newspaper.

"She may have the brain of a genius," he sighed. "But what good is it, to her or anybody else?"

Although they were talking about her, Helen showed no interest. For she had not heard them. An illness, when she was not quite two years old, had left her deaf, dumb, and blind. This meant that she must spend the rest of her life in silence and darkness. It was like being shut up in a black closet. No sound, no light could get in.

Helen slid off the chair and groped her way along the edge of a table to a cradle at her mother's feet. This had been Helen's cradle when she was a baby, and she loved to rock her doll in it.

But recently there had been a change in the Keller household that she could not understand. It disturbed her greatly. A baby girl, not much bigger than Helen's doll—but different, because it had arms and legs that moved—had come to live with the Kellers.

Since she could not hear anything, Helen did

not know the word "baby," nor any other words. She thought of her baby sister as "It." And she did not like "It," because often, when she tried to climb into her mother's lap, "It" would be there, and her mother's soft slender hands would push her gently away.

Now, as she reached the cradle and ran her hand inside, she found "It" there, snugly tucked in. Growling like an angry puppy, Helen ripped back the covers and tipped the cradle over, dumping the baby out. Fortunately, her mother caught the baby before she hit the floor. Quickly Captain Keller grabbed Helen by the shoulders and jerked her away, shaking her soundly.

"That settles it," he said sharply. "We're going to have to send her away to an institution!"

Helen's mother, still trembling with fright, began to cry.

"No—no—no!" she pleaded. "We can't do that to her! I've heard of those places—they're for feeble-minded children. They won't even try to teach her anything!"

Captain Keller, still holding on to Helen as she kicked and fought like a little wild animal, spoke more gently now.

"We've tried to teach her," he said, "but it's no use. And we can't keep her here. She's getting too big and strong. She's dangerous. She might have killed the baby!"

And Helen, in her rage and despair, kept crying to herself, over and over again, "Why are They doing this to me? Why? WHY?"

To Helen, since she knew no words, the people about her were all lumped together as "They" —her father, her mother, and the little colored girl, Martha Washington, who was her playmate.

And mostly "They" meant hands. Hands that pulled her back when she was about to run into something. Hands that caught her when she stumbled over something and kept her from falling. Hands that gave her things—and took them away from her. Hands that sometimes stroked her tumbled curls and comforted her. Hands that sometimes held her in a powerful grip, as her father's hands held her now, and would not let her get away.

She had to depend on her own small hands, too, to be both eyes and ears. Already she had learned many things through her sensitive little fingertips. They could find the first violets in the springtime, shyly nestling in the grass. They knew the round, smooth surfaces of eggs in a nest, and they had taught her not to drop the eggs or squeeze them too hard, for they would break. They knew the soft fur of a kitten and the silky coat of her setter dog, Belle.

Her restless, questioning little hands had explored her mother's face and had told her that sometimes those soft, smooth cheeks would be wet with tears. Helen did not know the word for tears—only that when she was in trouble and unhappy her own cheeks would be wet like that, too.

"Have They been doing bad things to you, too?" she would wonder.

Standing between her parents with her hands on their faces, she had felt their lips move. To her, it seemed that They were playing some queer sort of game They never played with her. She would move her lips, too. But They paid no attention.

"What are They doing?" she would ask herself. "Why don't They do it with me, too?"

She wanted so desperately to make them understand! But since she couldn't, she had learned to grab a thing when she wanted it, to push it roughly away when she didn't. And to fight like a little wildcat when big, strong hands tried to control her. Sometimes, because she was shut off from things and lonely, she would fly into rages which, as she grew bigger and stronger, really made her dangerous.

"Let me out of here!" she would cry inside

herself. "I've got to get out of here! I've GOT to!"

Now, when Helen's mother and father had finally succeeded in quieting her, they put her to bed. Returning to the living room, they sat down to talk about her, thoughtfully, sadly.

"It's no use," her father said. "We can't teach her anything."

"I know," her mother sighed. "We're letting her have her own way too much."

"But how can you punish a child," her father asked, "when you can't get through to her and make her understand why you're doing it?"

Her mother shook her head. Then she asked: "Why don't we write to that man in Boston that Dr. Bell told us about?"

Some months earlier Helen's parents had taken her to a famous eye doctor in Baltimore. He had not been able to help her, but he had suggested that they take her to Dr. Alexander Graham Bell in Washington.

"Perhaps Dr. Bell can do something about Helen's deafness," the eye doctor had said. "It was while trying to find some way to help deaf children that he invented the telephone, you know."

So the Kellers had taken their daughter to see Dr. Bell. He had held Helen on his lap and let her play with his watch while he sadly told her parents he could do nothing for her.

"But there's a man up in Boston, a Mr. Michael Anagnos, who runs a school for blind children," Dr. Bell had said. "It's called the Perkins Institution for the Blind.

"There's a woman living at the school, named Laura Bridgman, who is blind, deaf, and dumb like your little girl. I understand the people at the school have found a way of talking to her by spelling out words with their fingers in her hand.

"Maybe Mr. Anagnos could do something for Helen. Here's his address. I'll write it down for you."

Remembering all this, Captain Keller now looked at his wife doubtfully. He could not bear to think how heartbroken she would be if this, too, failed. But he could not resist the pleading expression in her eyes.

"All right," he said slowly. "We'll try. I'll write to Mr. Anagnos tomorrow."

2.

The Stranger

HELEN HAD no way of knowing that this day, March 3, 1887, would be the most important day in her whole life.

Six months had passed since the evening when she had tipped her baby sister out of the cradle. As he had promised, her father had written to Mr. Anagnos. And today Miss Anne Sullivan, only twenty years old and just out of school, was arriving from Boston to live with the Kellers and be Helen's teacher.

Of course Helen knew nothing about Miss Sullivan's expected arrival. But she had sensed for several days that something unusual was going on.

For one thing, she had noticed that one of the rooms upstairs, usually kept closed and smelling musty, had been opened and aired.

Martha Washington's mother had been in there, too, with broom and dustcloth. And this morning the bed had been made up with clean sheets. Fresh towels, smelling sweet, like the linen closet, had been placed on the rack.

In the kitchen Martha Washington's mother was busy with extra cooking. She baked a cake and let Helen lick the pan in which she made the frosting. But even this treat failed to bring much pleasure to an anxious, unhappy little girl.

Round and round inside her head raced the questions she could not put into words.

"Something's going to happen. But what? Why can't I know? Why? Why? *Why?*"

And because she could get no answers, she was restless and cross and badly behaved.

Now she had followed her mother out onto the porch and was standing beside her, tense and worried.

Mrs. Keller was about to go to the station to meet Miss Sullivan. Helen of course did not know that. But her mother had on her hat and coat. That meant she was going somewhere. And Helen wanted to go along.

Soon Helen's father came out on the porch, holding a letter from Mr. Anagnos, which he had read over and over again.

"Mr. Anagnos writes that Miss Sullivan was

blind, too, when she was a child," he said, "but they were able to operate on her eyes."

"I wish they could operate on Helen's eyes," his wife remarked wistfully as she drew on her gloves. But Captain Keller sighed and shook his head.

"This is a different kind of blindness," he said sadly. "An operation would do no good."

Suddenly Helen stiffened. She knew that the horses and carriage were being brought around from the stable. The clump-clump-clumping of horses' hoofs shook the porch ever so slightly. Not enough so that the average person would notice it. But Helen could feel it in her feet. She had learned to be alert for signs like this.

She grabbed hold of her mother's coat and tried to follow her into the carriage. But her father's big, strong hands pulled her back.

Sobbing and making little sounds like a hurt puppy, Helen broke away and stumbled down the driveway after the carriage. Her father hurried after her and caught her. Reaching into his pocket, he brought out some peppermint drops. Helen ate them, but they did not make her any happier. Slowly she found her way back to the porch.

She was hardly an attractive little girl as she stood there in the spring sunshine, waiting.

Her light brown hair had not been combed

that day and was full of tangles. Sometimes, when she was in a bad mood as she was today, she would not let anyone comb her hair or wash her face. Her mother, who hated to spank her, because she was so sorry for her, would just give in to her. And now her grimy little face was streaked with tears.

Finally after what seemed to Helen a very long time, she felt the porch shake ever so slightly again under her feet. The horses and carriage were coming up the driveway.

Then Helen felt someone coming toward her. Nearer. Nearer. With a little growl she lunged forward—into a strange pair of arms.

Desperately she jerked herself loose. This stranger was no bigger than her mother. But the arms were stronger, the hands more firm. And the smell. It was not the sweet smell of those little silk bags her mother kept in her bureau drawers. Helen remembered this smell from the time her parents had taken her on the train to Baltimore to see the eye doctor—the smell of cinders and coal smoke.

"We are glad, Miss Sullivan, that you have come to be our little girl's teacher," Captain Keller was saying.

But Helen of course could not hear him. If she had known any words, she would have called this newcomer The Stranger. For that was what

she was to Helen. And she would continue to be
The Stranger for what would seem to both of
them a long, long time.

Helen brushed against a traveling bag and
grabbed it. Sometimes there was candy in traveling bags! The Stranger gently started to take
the bag away. But Helen hurled herself at her
with such force that they both would have fallen,
had not Captain Keller caught them.

Curious now, in spite of her resentment,
Helen followed The Stranger upstairs into the
room that had been made ready for her. The
Stranger opened the traveling bag, firmly pushing Helen's dirty little hands away.

She brought out a doll and placed it in Helen's
arms. Smiling, she watched as Helen delightedly
ran her fingers over it and held it lovingly
against her check.

Then she gently led the child across the room
and placed her small right hand, palm up, on a
table. Slowly she moved her own fingers inside
Helen's palm.

She repeated the motions several times while
Helen waited, curious about this new game.
Then she guided Helen's small fingers through
the same motions, spelling the word over and
over: D-O-L-L, D-O-L-L, D-O-L-L. Then Helen
tried it without help several times, clumsily at
first, then perfectly.

Next, The Stranger started to take the doll away from Helen. She intended to give the doll back again if Helen spelled the word once more with her fingers.

But Helen did not understand. The motions, spelling the word D-O-L-L, had no meaning for her. The doll was being taken away from her, as so many things were.

Savagely she leaped at The Stranger, trying to grab the doll. But she could not get it. Groping wildly, she found the door and ran out, slamming it behind her.

The Stranger did not try to find her. Instead, she went on unpacking her bag, smiling thoughtfully as she did so.

"We've had our first lesson, little Helen," she said to herself. "It was only half successful. But that wasn't your fault. I was going too fast for you. But you *can* learn. I *know* you can!"

3.

Helen Has a Tantrum

BEFORE SHE could be taught anything else, Helen would have to learn obedience. The Stranger realized this from the start.

Partly because Helen's parents were sorry for her and partly because they did not know how to go about it, they had never really tried to make her mind. The result was that whenever Helen could not have her own way she would fly into a rage, and nobody could manage her.

"But I'm strong, too, young lady," The Stranger thought. "And I can be just as stubborn as you are."

Their first real battle came at the breakfast table a couple of mornings after The Stranger arrived.

Helen's table manners were very bad. She did

not even know how to eat with a spoon. Instead of sitting in her place and eating from her own plate, she was allowed to run around the table, grabbing from other people's plates whatever smelled good to her.

When she was very small, people had thought this was amusing. It was like feeding a puppy at the table. Now that she was almost seven, her parents had grown used to it. When she snatched food from their plates they would go on talking as if nothing out of the ordinary was happening.

But this morning Helen made a sudden dive at The Stranger's plate and started to grab a handful of scrambled eggs. The Stranger pushed her greasy little hand away. And when Helen tried again, she slapped her.

Helen threw herself on the floor, kicking and screaming with rage.

While Mr. and Mrs. Keller looked on in horrified silence, The Stranger pulled the child up off the floor, shook her, and set her down, hard, on her chair. Helen squirmed and kicked, but The Stranger's hands held her in a firm grip.

"Don't worry—it's just a tantrum!" The Stranger panted as she noted the expression on the faces of Helen's parents.

She finally managed to get a spoon into Helen's hand. Holding it firmly there, she showed her how to scoop up the scrambled eggs

onto the spoon. Then she tried to guide it up to
Helen's mouth. But Helen angrily jerked her
hand away and threw the spoon on the floor.

Without a word The Stranger dragged Helen
off the chair. Firmly holding onto her hand, she
guided it to the spoon and made her pick it up.
Then she set her down hard on the chair again.

Helen was now crying. She could not understand why this was being done. It had never
happened to her before.

Captain Keller threw down his napkin and
got up from the table.

"I've had all of this I can stand," he growled,
and he went stamping out of the room. Helen's
mother followed him.

The Stranger went over and locked the door
behind them. Then she returned to her breakfast, although every mouthful choked her.

"We've got to have this battle sometime," she
told herself. "It might as well be now."

Helen began to pinch her. And each time she
did it The Stranger slapped her.

Next Helen slid down off her chair and felt
her way around the table. But there was no one
at her mother's place nor her father's.

Quietly now, because she was puzzled, she
found her way back to The Stranger. She did not
try to grab anything this time. But placing her

hand on The Stranger's wrist, she felt it being raised and lowered. The Stranger was eating.

Again The Stranger placed the spoon in Helen's hand and guided it up to her mouth. And this time Helen let her do it. Being very hungry, she finished her breakfast without any more bursts of temper.

As soon as she had finished, Helen jerked off the napkin that had been tied around her neck and threw it on the floor. Then she slid off her chair and ran over to the door.

Discovering that she could not open it, she flew into another rage, pounding on the door. The Stranger came over, but she did not open the door.

Instead, she firmly led the howling, kicking Helen back to the table and forced her to pick up the napkin off the floor. She started to show her how to fold it. But Helen threw the napkin on the floor again and herself on top of it.

This time, instead of pulling her up, The Stranger let her alone and went on with her own breakfast—even harder to eat now, because it was stone cold.

Helen could not understand this. And because she couldn't she was even more angry. She tried several times to jerk The Stranger's chair out from under her. That was impossible, so she broke into a violent fit of sobbing. Everything was going wrong this morning! But *why?*

"I hate you! I hate you! I hate you!" she kept crying inside herself. "Why are you doing this to me?"

And The Stranger, looking down at her, was saying softly, "Poor little girl! I'm not happy about this either. But you've got to learn to mind me. Otherwise I can't do anything for you."

The morning wore on. Again and again Helen ran to the door, found it locked, and threw herself on the floor kicking and howling with rage.

"I'll just have to let you wear yourself out," The Stranger sighed.

Again and again she tried to make Helen pick up the napkin, but Helen fought her off.

Helen's father left for his office. "I have a good notion to send that Yankee woman back to Boston," he snapped as he went out the door.

Helen's mother hurried upstairs, to the room farthest away from the dining room, so she could not hear the noise.

Martha Washington's mother was beginning to wonder if she would ever be able to get into the dining room to clear away the dirty dishes and set the table for lunch.

Finally Helen's anger left her, and she lay

on the floor quiet, her tear-stained face cradled in her arms.

Gently The Stranger bent over her and stroked her tumbled curls. Then she placed the napkin in Helen's hand once more and lifted her up to the table.

Without any struggle, Helen let The Stranger guide her hands. They folded the napkin and laid it on the table. Then The Stranger led her over to the door and opened it.

A very much subdued little girl wandered out onto the porch and on into the sunny garden.

The Stranger, starting wearily up the stairs, met Mrs. Keller on the landing.

"She finished her breakfast and folded her napkin," The Stranger said. But there was no triumph in her voice.

Back in her own room, she threw herself on the bed and cried herself to sleep.

4.

The Word Game

THE BATTLE of the Breakfast Table was the longest and one of the most violent of Helen's tussles with The Stranger. But it was by no means the last one.

After living with the Kellers for a week, Miss Sullivan decided that she could not help Helen unless she could take her away from her parents for a while. In order to make the child mind she was often forced to punish her, and Helen's parents constantly interfered. Especially her father, who could not bear to see his little girl cry.

Helen very quickly sensed the fact that her parents were on her side. And she would run to them every time The Stranger tried to discipline her.

The Stranger and Mrs. Keller were talking about this as they sat on the porch watching Helen at play in the garden.

"We can't help interfering," Mrs. Keller said. "We feel so sorry for the poor little thing."

The Stranger's reply was quick and urgent.

"Helen doesn't need your pity," she said. "She needs your help!"

"But what can we do?" Mrs. Keller sighed.

"I have an idea that might work," The Stranger answered, "if only you can persuade Captain Keller to agree to it. If I had Helen alone with me for a while, I think I could teach her to obey me. But now she can run to you every time I try to make her mind.

"I want her to learn to trust me and like me, as well as to obey. But this is impossible so long as she looks upon me as an outsider who makes her do things you don't make her do."

Mrs. Keller nodded.

"We own a cottage, about a quarter of a mile from here," she said. "You must have noticed it when you were out walking. It's tiny, but could be made comfortable. Perhaps you and Helen could stay there awhile."

"Just the thing!" The Stranger agreed. And Mrs. Keller promised to speak to her husband about the matter that evening.

At first Captain Keller did not think much of the idea. "Helen will be homesick," he predicted. "Poor little thing! Being away from us might even make her ill!" But his wife was so anxious to try Miss Sullivan's plan that at last he reluctantly agreed.

The following afternoon Helen was taken for a drive, which she loved. But this time she did not return home. Instead, she found herself in an unfamiliar place, alone with The Stranger.

She accepted it quietly at first. "They'll come and get me," she told herself. They always had before.

When bedtime came, however, this hope vanished. Helen was used to sleeping in her own small bed, alone. It was bad enough to have to get into this wide, unfamiliar bed. But when The Stranger started to get in with her, Helen rebelled.

"No! No! No!" she cried fiercely inside herself. "I won't have you close to me! I won't! I won't! I hate you! Go away!"

She hurled herself out of the bed, and it took The Stranger two hours to get her back. Finally, Helen fell asleep from sheer exhaustion, as close to the edge of the bed as she could get. The Stranger wearily crawled in on the other side.

"Perhaps they should have brought her own bed down here," The Stranger thought. "But

it might have confused her. She's got to learn
to accept changes. Dear God, help me to make it
easy for her!"

In the days that followed Helen was so busy
that she began to forget a little, her dislike of
The Stranger. There were so many interesting
things to do!

First The Stranger gave her some beads and
a string. The beads were of different shapes and
sizes. Some were made of wood, some of glass.

Helen's sensitive little fingers very quickly
learned to string the beads and to sort them
out into piles. The Stranger started a more com-
plicated string for her—so many beads from
one pile, so many from another. Helen learned
to do that too with surprising ease.

"This is fun!" she told herself. And for the
first time since they had been alone, The Stranger saw her smile.

The next game was harder. And because it
was harder, it was more interesting. The Stranger gave her a ball of yarn and a crochet hook.
Holding Helen's hands in her own, she showed
her how to loop the yarn in and out, over and
under the hook, making a chain.

Helen was fascinated. But she made many
mistakes at first. Forgetting that she didn't like
The Stranger, she went back to her again and
again to find out what was wrong.

"I *can* do this!" she kept telling herself. "I'll *do* it!"

She kept at it until one day she had made a chain that stretched almost all the way across the room. She smiled with pleasure when The Stranger rewarded her with a piece of cake. And she did not jerk away when she felt The Stranger's hand patting her shoulder approvingly.

But most interesting of all was the game they played with their hands. Helen had no way of knowing, of course, but The Stranger actually was teaching her the Manual Alphabet.

The Manual Alphabet, which is shown on page 159, is a sign language. It was developed many years ago so that deaf and dumb people can talk with their hands.

As you see when you examine it, each position of the fingers means a different letter.

Learning to talk with the Manual Alphabet is not too difficult if you can see. You simply spell out the words with your fingers. In fact, it can be fun—a secret language!

But since Helen could not see, the only way she could learn the Manual Alphabet was for someone to make the letters in her hand. With her fingers she could learn the different positions, each one a letter. Then with her own fingers she could make the letters.

This would have been a very slow, tedious, almost hopeless task, had not Helen's mind been so quick. Far from being feeble-minded, as some of her elders had suspected, she was an exceptionally bright child. And she had a remarkable memory. In a few days she learned how to make almost every letter in the Manual Alphabet. She was not learning them, however, as separate letters, in order: A, B, C, and so on. Instead, she learned them grouped together in words.

She learned how to make new words every day. For instance, C-A-K-E. W-A-T-E-R. C-U-P. H-E-L-E-N. P-A-P-A. M-A-M-A. B-A-B-Y.

But so far, these words had no meaning for her at all. It was just a game.

"I'm pretty good at it," she would think. "It's fun!"

And The Stranger, patiently going over the same words with her day after day, would look at her and think:

"Some day these words will unlock the door to your prison, little Helen. I don't know when or how. But they will. They *must!*"

Every morning on his way to the office Helen's father would stand outside, looking in the window to see how she was getting along. Helen, of course, did not know he was there.

"How quiet she is!" he often exclaimed as he

watched her contentedly playing with her beads or her crochet hook. "She's not like the same child at all!"

One morning he brought Helen's dog Belle into the cottage. Helen greeted the dog with a little cry of delight and a big hug. Then she sat down on the floor, picked up one of Belle's paws, and began to move her claws about, this way and that.

"What on earth is she doing to the dog?" her father asked as he and The Strange both stared. Suddenly The Stranger, watching Helen's fingers, smiled broadly.

"Look—she's teaching the dog to spell!" she said. "She's trying to get her to spell *DOLL!*"

But Captain Keller shook his head in discouragement.

"What's the good of it?" he demanded. "She doesn't know the meaning of the word. It's just a game."

The Stranger's expression was pleading, as she said quietly, "She'll learn the meaning. Give her a little more time—just a little more time."

5.

W-A-T-E-R

THE DAY had got off to a bad start. It was April 5th, just two days over a month since The Stranger had come to be Helen's teacher.

Because Captain Keller had insisted on it, Helen and The Stranger had moved out of the cottage. He wanted his little girl at home. Now he and Helen's mother were learning the Manual Alphabet. But Captain Keller wasn't trying very hard.

"What's the use?" he kept saying.

"You're going to need it," The Stranger told him. "Sooner or later—and I believe it will be before very long—Helen will know the meaning of words. And then you can talk to her, with your fingers in her hand."

Helen was now much quieter and better behaved than she had been. Everybody noticed it. She did not have so many tantrums. And when she did have one it did not last very long.

But sometimes, as on this April morning, she would wake up feeling out of sorts and cross. For one thing, she was getting bored with the word game.

"I know all that," she would think impatiently. "Why don't we play something else?"

All the morning The Stranger had been spelling two words into Helen's hand, W-A-T-E-R, and C-U-P. She would spell C-U-P and give her a cup to hold. Then she would pour a little water into the cup, dip Helen's fingers into it, and wait hopefully for Helen to spell back, W-A-T-E-R.

But Helen, not understanding, would spell C-U-P.

"What is it you want?" she kept thinking. "I'd do it if I knew. But I don't know. Can't you see I'm trying?"

"Poor child, you're getting tired," The Stranger said as Helen jerked her hand away and nearly upset the cup. "Let's rest awhile. Here!"

And she handed her the new doll she had brought her from Boston. Helen played with the doll awhile, but she was thinking of the word game.

"What do you want?" she kept saying to herself. "Why can't I do it? I try and try!"

Presently The Stranger started in on the word game again. C-U-P. W-A-T-E-R. But Helen kept getting more and more mixed up and irritable. Finally she seized her doll and dashed it to the floor. Its head broke in half a dozen pieces.

With grim satisfaction she followed with her hands The Stranger's motions as she swept up the broken pieces.

"I don't care!" Helen told herself fiercely. "I don't care the least little bit! Why don't you leave me alone?"

She gave a little sigh of relief when The Stranger brought her hat to her. They were going outdoors. No more of that stupid game.

Although Helen did not know it, The Stranger carried the cup in her hand as they walked down the path toward the pump house.

Helen raised her head and sniffed with pleasure. That sweet smell! Although she didn't know the word for it, it was honeysuckle. She reached out her hand and touched the vine lovingly as they passed.

Someone was pumping water. The Stranger led Helen to the pump, placed the cup in her hand again, and held it under the spout.

Helen's first impulse was to throw the cup

away. But she liked the sensation as the cool water flowed down over her hand into the cup. So she held it there, smiling a little.

The Stranger took hold of her other hand and began to spell the word again. W-A-T-E-R. Slowly at first. Then faster. Over and over again.

Suddenly Helen dropped the cup. She stood absolutely still, rigid, hardly breathing. Inside her mind, a new thought spun round and round:

"W-A-T-E-R! W-A-T-E-R! This lovely, cool stuff. W-A-T-E-R?"

Wildly she groped for The Stranger's hand. Her trembling little fingers began, W-A-T—? She had not finished when she felt The Stranger's pat of approval on her shoulder. She was right! That was it!

For the first time in her life Helen Keller had "talked" with another human being!

The Stranger's eyes were wet as she cried: "Helen, you've got it! You've *got* it!"

Helen could not hear her. But that did not matter. For now another idea came flashing into her mind.

If that stuff was W-A-T-E-R, what about the other games they played with their hands?

She reached down and touched the ground, then turned eagerly to The Stranger. Her heart pounding like a little hammer, she felt The Stranger's fingers moving in her hand.

Several times The Stranger's fingers spelled the word, Helen intently following every movement. Then she spelled it back. G-R-O-U-N-D. She had it fixed in her memory now. She would not forget.

Now she must find out about more things. Fast! She ran about, touching everything she could reach. The Stranger's fingers told her: V-I-N-E, P-U-M-P, T-R-E-L-L-I-S.

Helen bumped into the nurse, who was coming into the pump house carrying Helen's baby sister, Mildred, whom she still thought of as "It." She touched "It" and ran back to The Stranger. B-A-B-Y! It had been spelled into her hand many, many times. Now it had meaning. Little Mildred was no longer just a thing called "It."

Suddenly Helen stood still, thinking hard. Then she reached out toward The Stranger.

Although she could not put it into words, as you or I would, her hand grasping The Stranger's hand asked a question:

"Who are you?"

And into her eager little palm the word came back: T-E-A-C-H-E-R.

In that warm, glowing moment all the hostility Helen had felt toward The Stranger melted away. For no longer was she a stranger. She was Teacher.

T-E-A-C-H-E-R! To Helen Keller, the most important word she would ever learn. And to Anne Sullivan, the most beautiful.

6.

Everything Has a Name!

WHEN Captain Keller came home from his office that evening, his wife and little daughter met him at the door. There was nothing unusual about this. But when he lifted Helen in his arms to kiss her, something unusual did happen. Something he would never forget as long as he lived.

Helen squirmed and reached out eagerly for Teacher, who was standing near by. Swiftly Teacher's fingers moved in her small palm.

A smile lighted up Helen's face. She knew those finger movements! She had felt them in her hand dozens of times. And she knew how to make them, too! Quickly her own fingers started to move.

"What's that?" her father asked. "What's she trying to spell now?"

Mrs. Keller's voice trembled with excitement as she cried, "Arthur, it's 'Papa'! She's saying 'Papa' with her fingers!"

Both trying to talk at once, Mrs. Keller and Teacher told him what had happened at the pump. And how Helen had been running about ever since touching things, and running back to Teacher to find out what they were.

Captain Keller was unable to speak as he held out his hand to Teacher. But his grip, so hard that it almost crushed her fingers, told her what he could not say. And that evening he started learning the Manual Alphabet—in earnest.

It was a long day for Helen. Everything had a name! Everything! And she wanted to learn them all at once. By bedtime she knew the meaning of more than thirty words. Every one of them she had learned by following intently the movements of Teacher's fingers in her hand.

It was also the first really happy day she had ever known. At bedtime a radiant little girl put her arms around Teacher and kissed her good night. It was the first time Helen ever kissed Teacher. And the first time she let Teacher kiss her.

For the time being Helen would be content with this thrilling adventure—learning the names of things.

But Teacher faced a problem. What to do next!

"I have no training for this job," she sighed as she tossed and turned that night unable to go to sleep. "There are so many, many things I don't know!"

Staring into the dark, Anne Sullivan thought of her own childhood. It had been little more promising than Helen's had up to now. In one way it had been worse.

Helen had a comfortable home and a father and mother who loved her. They would have given anything in the world to make it possible for her to see and hear like other children.

But little Annie Sullivan's mother had died when she was eight. And two years later her father had deserted Anne, whose eyes were bad, and her little brother Jimmie, who had a diseased hip.

Nobody wanted to undertake the care of a ten-year-old girl who was going blind or a little boy who was a cripple. So the two children had been sent to a poorhouse at Tewksbury, Massachusetts.

They were the only children in the place. The other inmates were old people, who had been sent there because they could no longer work, and had no money and no friends. Most of them were physically ill. Some were mentally ill.

Jimmie had died in the poorhouse. But after four years, Annie, who had become almost totally blind, was rescued and sent to the school for blind children in Boston, run by Mr. Anagnos.

Until that time, Annie had had no schooling whatever. She had not even learned to spell her own name. So, at Perkins Institution, she had to start in the first grade, although she was fourteen years old. And the little children, who couldn't understand what such a big girl was doing in their class, made fun of her.

About a year later a doctor had operated on her eyes. Her sight had improved so greatly that she had learned to read and write as most people do, though her eyes were still very weak.

Mr. Anagnos, head of the Perkins School, had chosen her to be little Helen Keller's teacher for four principal reasons. Anne Sullivan had been blind herself and knew what it was like. She knew how to read raised print with her fingers as blind people do. She knew how to use the Manual Alphabet. And she liked children.

Now, as she lay in bed trying to sleep, she decided that, since she herself had had such a miserable childhood, she must see that Helen had a happy one.

"Please don't let anybody call her a poor little thing any more," she begged Helen's parents, next day. "She's not a poor little thing.

She's a strong, healthy child. I suspect she has a better mind than many children who can see and hear. But if she ever got to feeling sorry for herself, she'd be lost.

"And let's not discourage her when she wants to try to do things—even if we think she can't. She may surprise us!"

One of the first things Teacher wanted to do was to teach Helen how to play like other children. To run and skip and jump. In places where there was nothing for Helen to run into or knock over she romped with her, playing rough tomboy games.

"Don't worry," she reassured Helen's mother. "She'll take some bumps. But she'll learn how to handle herself. We don't want her to go groping around all the rest of her life, always afraid of running into something or falling!"

One thing Teacher noticed was that Helen never laughed. She asked Mrs. Keller about it.

"Helen has never laughed since she was a baby, before she was ill," Mrs. Keller said sadly. "I guess she's forgotten how."

"Perhaps I can help her to remember," thought Teacher. And one day when they were playing tag in the garden, she caught Helen and tickled her.

Then to Helen's father and mother, sitting on

the porch, came a sound they had never expected to hear again.

"It's Helen," Mrs. Keller said in wonder, her voice hardly above a whisper. "She's laughing! She's *laughing!*"

7.

Learning Is Fun

HELEN WAS now learning new words every day, as fast as Teacher's fingers could spell them into her hand. But she did not yet know how to use them—to put them into sentences. Teacher talked the problem over with Mrs. Keller.

"How did we learn to talk when we were little?" she asked. "By hearing people talk, of course! Helen will learn the same way—through our fingers in her hand."

Mrs. Keller nodded. "But it will be very slow, won't it?" she asked.

"It may be faster than we think," Teacher replied. "Helen's quick at catching on. At first, of course, she won't understand everything we spell into her hand. She'll get only the words she knows. But they will give her a clue, and I be-

51

lieve she'll soon begin to figure things out. We might as well start work on that this morning."

So far, Helen knew only nouns—the names of things. Before she could make sentences she would have to learn how to use verbs—"is," for instance, "run" and "walk" and "come" and "go." And prepositions—"in" and "on" and "to" and "from."

Now Teacher gave her some cards on which were printed in large, raised letters some words she knew—B-O-X, T-A-B-L-E, H-E-L-E-N, C-L-O-S-E-T, and so on.

She let Helen run her fingers over them. And as Helen felt each word, Teacher spelled it into her hand. The little girl quickly understood. Those bumps under her fingertips meant the same things as the movements of Teacher's fingers in her hand. And each set of bumps had a different meaning.

She was greatly pleased with herself, and her eager grab at Teacher's hand meant something she couldn't yet put into a sentence:

"Let's play some more!"

Next Teacher gave her some cards with bumps on them that Helen did not understand. I-S, and O-N. Teacher did not try to explain them. Instead, she invented a fascinating new game.

She put a box on a table. Next she placed the

card with the word B-O-X, on the box. Then she put the card with the word, T-A-B-L-E, on the table. Between them she placed the cards with the words, I-S and O-N.

Helen ran her fingers over them. She was puzzled when she felt the words, I-S and O-N. But she smiled with delight when she recognized the familiar B-O-X and T-A-B-L-E.

It was a wonderful game, and Helen and Teacher played it by the hour, with different cards and new words. Helen never grew tired of it.

"She's so eager to learn!" Teacher told Mrs. Keller one day. "Come and see what she has done now."

She led Helen's mother into the child's room. The closet door was open, and in the closet stood Helen. She had pinned on her dress the card for H-E-L-E-N. And lying on the floor beside her were the cards, I-S, I-N, and C-L-O-S-E-T. H-E-L-E-N I-S I-N C-L-O-S-E-T!

"She worked it out all by herself," Teacher said proudly. "It's her first sentence!"

Long before the end of April, Helen was making sentences regularly. Some of them were pretty badly mixed up and funny. But Teacher's fingers in her hand could always set her straight.

While she was learning to make sentences with the cards, Helen was also learning to read, as she had learned to use the Manual Alphabet, whole words at a time.

Teacher sent to Boston for some little books, short, simple stories in raised print. Helen's eager little fingers raced through them, and she was delighted when she found words she knew. The little books also helped her to learn new words.

Never did any little girl have a more delightful playmate than Teacher. Helen thought everything they did was fun. In the lovely spring weather they spent most of their time outdoors. There were no regular hours for lessons, but there were lessons all the time—lessons that, to Helen, were games.

The Kellers lived on a farm on the outskirts of Tuscumbia. Teacher took Helen to the fields where the men were plowing and sowing seeds. She let her feel the upturned earth, warm in the sun. And she gave her some seeds and showed her how to put them into the ground. Later they returned to the fields, and taking Helen's hand, Teacher "showed" her the tiny plants coming up.

It was the time of year when things were being born. Little colts, calves, lambs, puppies. One day Teacher placed in Helen's arms a fat, wriggling baby pig. Then she held Helen's fingers against its throat so she could feel the vibration when the pig squealed.

Most thrilling of all to Helen was the time when Teacher gave her an egg to hold and let her feel a baby chick pecking its way out of the shell!

But it was almost as thrilling when Teacher taught her to climb trees. At first Teacher guided Helen's hands and feet from branch to branch. Confident that Teacher would not let her fall, the little girl was not afraid. She and Teacher had a favorite tree and spent many happy hours high up in its friendly branches, while Helen ran her fingers through the little books from Boston.

One sultry morning, coming home from a walk, they climbed up into the tree and found it delightfully cool. Teacher decided they would have their lunch there. By now Helen understood what Teacher meant when she spelled into her hand: "Wait. Teacher will come back."

Leaving Helen in the tree, Teacher hurried into the house to get some sandwiches.

She was gone longer than she had intended, however. And before long Helen knew a storm was coming up. She knew the sky was black because the heat, which meant sunshine to her, had gone out of the air. And she could tell that it was going to rain by the smell that came up from the earth.

Suddenly the branches began to whip about as gusts of wind hit the tree. A shiver ran through the child as she clung with all her might to the big branch on which she was sitting. Small twigs snapped, and leaves blew away.

The whole earth jarred with a clap of thunder which Helen could not hear but could feel. For a moment she was terrified. Then, just as it started to rain, she felt Teacher's strong, comforting arms about her. She was safe!

For several days after that, they did not climb any trees. Teacher realized that Helen had been badly frightened.

But early one morning Helen went out into the garden alone. At once she was attracted by the fragrance of its blossoms to a mimosa tree that grew some distance from the house.

She wandered down to the tree and stood near it. Then, after a moment's hesitation, she felt around and placed her foot on one of the low branches. Although she had never climbed this tree before, she felt her way to the next branch and the next.

"There!" she said to herself as she settled triumphantly in a seat someone had built high up in the tree. "I'll never be afraid to do this again!"

8.

Helen Writes a Letter

IT WAS a hot, sticky summer morning, not quite three months after Helen had first learned at the pump that words had meaning. Helen was bored and wanted Teacher to go for a walk with her. But Teacher said no—it was too hot.

She handed Helen one of the reading books to play with. But Helen's fingertips soon found all the words she knew. Impatiently she put the book down. Now she didn't know what to do with herself. She stood beside Teacher and nudged her elbow.

All morning Teacher had been hunched over her desk, writing a letter. Because her eyes were so weak, it was slow, hard work. And Helen wasn't making it any easier.

Finally, when Helen nudged her elbow again

—and nearly upset the ink bottle—Teacher laid down her pen and frowned.

"Little rascal!" she thought. "What am I going to do with her!"

Then she took Helen's hand and patiently spelled into it, as she had several times before, "Go away. Teacher is writing a letter."

Helen knew what a letter was. Several times they had gone to the post office, and Teacher had given her a letter and shown her how to drop it into the mail chute.

Helen wasn't quite sure what the word "writing" meant, though. But whatever it was, Teacher was doing it, and she wanted to do it, too. So she nudged Teacher's elbow again. And her fingers spelled rapidly:

"Helen—letter. Helen—letter."

That gave Teacher an idea. She got up from her desk and went over to her closet, with Helen tagging at her heels. From the top shelf she pulled down a box.

With Helen's hand on her wrist following every movement, she took out of the box a piece of thick, heavy cardboard, about the size of a sheet of writing paper. It had lines across it, like the lines on the pages in a school tablet. Only these lines were not printed. They were indented, in grooves, so that they could be felt with the fingers. This piece of cardboard was a writing board.

Teacher handed it to Helen and guided her fingers along the grooved lines. Then she put a piece of paper over the writing board, pressed the paper down into the grooves, and had Helen run her fingers over it again, finding the lines.

Next she gave Helen a pencil and guided her hand while Helen made some marks between the lines. Helen didn't know it, but she was printing the words:

"Cat does drink milk."

They did this several times, always keeping the marks between the lines. Then Helen pulled her hand away, which meant:

"Let me do it!"

Teacher smiled and went on with her letter. When she finished it and looked around, Helen had disappeared. As Teacher was about to go in search of the child, Mrs. Keller came into the room with a folded piece of paper.

"Helen brought this to me," she said. "And she keeps trying to say something about a letter."

Over and over on the paper Helen had printed the words about the cat drinking milk. Her printing was uneven—the letters slanted in all directions. But they could be read. And they were between the lines.

"Well," said Teacher, "if she is that anxious to write, she may as well begin to learn."

Again Teacher brought the box down off the closet shelf. And this time she took out several pieces of cardboard. These had big raised letters on them that looked somewhat like ordinary print, except that they were made entirely with straight lines. Most of them were square. Even "O." And "Q."

"This is the Square-Hand Alphabet, which is used to teach blind children to write," Teacher explained to Mrs. Keller. "The letters are square because, when you can't see what you're doing, it's easier to draw straight lines than curves."

So far, in learning to use the Manual Alphabet and to read from her books and cards, Helen had not broken words up into separate letters. When she came across a word she knew, like "box," she didn't spell it out, "B-O-X." Her fingertips took in the whole word.

Each set of bumps on a card or in the book meant a word, just as did each set of motions made by Teacher's fingers in her hand.

She had learned that you must put words together to make a sentence. Now she was to learn that you must put letters together to make a word.

Teacher started with the word, "box," which

was short and easy to remember. She fitted the three Square-Hand letters into a frame and let Helen study them with her fingertips.

"This is B-O-X," Teacher explained, "just as you find it on the card."

Then she placed Helen's left hand on the letters, so that she could follow them with her fingertips. And she guided her right hand with the pencil as Helen printed the word in Square-Hand letters on the paper placed on the writing board.

It did not take Helen long to understand what she was doing. After all, the Square-Hand letters weren't very different from the raised letters on the cards and in the books.

Helen was fascinated with this new game. She spent so many hours at it that she got a callus on her finger from gripping the pencil so hard. Sometimes Teacher had to drag her outdoors for the walks she loved so much.

In the meantime the little girl was learning new words every day and learning how to use them in sentences. And as she learned new words she learned how to print them.

Finally one day she handed Teacher a piece of paper folded like a letter. Her little fingers fairly danced as they spelled:

"Helen write letter!"

The letter didn't make much sense. Helen had

simply strung together all the sentences she had learned how to print. There were no capital letters, no commas, no periods.

But it was written less than a week after the child had printed her first word, "box." And her seventh birthday was still ten days away.

9.

Another Way of Writing

LEARNING to write with a pencil was hard work, and it kept Helen busy for several days. But she was not satisfied. For she had found out that there was another way of writing. Teacher used it sometimes. And Helen wanted to learn to do it, too.

Helen made her discovery one morning when she found Teacher punching holes through a little metal frame with a stiletto.

Helen still did not know how to ask questions very well. It was early in June, and Teacher had been with her only since March. But when Helen put her hand on Teacher's wrist and held it there, Teacher knew she was asking, "What are you doing?"

Teacher put down the stiletto and spelled into Helen's hand:

"Wait a minute, and I'll show you."

While Helen waited, very curious now, Teacher punched some more holes, drew a piece of heavy paper out of the frame, and laid it aside. Then she handed the frame to Helen.

The frame was made of two strips of metal, about the size of the small rulers children carry in their school bags. The two strips were connected at one end with a hinge. In the top strip of metal there were little holes, and in the bottom strip dents that matched the holes above them.

Teacher took the frame back. She fitted a heavy piece of paper inside, clamped the two strips together, like a waffle iron, and gave it back to Helen.

"Here," she spelled into Helen's hand. "You may play with it."

Then she gave Helen the stiletto and showed her how to punch it through the little holes.

After Helen had punched several times, Teacher opened the frame and took out the piece of paper. She turned the paper over and let Helen feel the raised dots. These had been made by the tip of the stiletto, punching through the holes and pressing the paper down into the dents below.

Helen was fascinated and spent some time punching the stiletto through the little holes, taking out the paper and feeling the raised dots she had made.

But there was still something she wanted to know. And her hand on Teacher's wrist asked another question:

"What's it for?"

"It's another way of writing," Teacher's fingers told her. Helen was puzzled. But she went on punching holes. She knew what writing meant. It meant writing letters.

"But what a funny way to write letters!" she thought.

Still—most of the things she had learned from Teacher had seemed odd to her at first. But they were interesting and fun. This was, too. So she went on punching until there was no more room on the paper.

She reached out for Teacher, but Teacher had left. Helen thought she knew where to find her, however. She went downstairs and out on the porch, and there were Mama and Teacher, rocking and fanning themselves. It was very hot.

Eagerly Helen handed Teacher the paper covered with raised dots, and her small fingers danced as they spelled: "Letter!"

Teacher was surprised. "I didn't think she knew I was writing a letter," she said to Mrs. Keller. "Well, I'll start teaching her to read and write Braille. But not until she has had more practice writing with a pencil.''

Teacher waited several weeks, until the end of July. Then she started teaching Helen Braille, the written language of the blind.

Braille is a language written entirely in dots —raised dots on heavy paper, which the blind can follow easily with their sensitive fingertips. Each group of dots means a letter.

''One dot means 'a,' the same 'a' you make with your pencil,'' Teacher spelled carefully into Helen's hand. ''Two dots mean 'b.' ''

Helen understood at once and soon learned the whole Braille Alphabet. She was delighted when Teacher gave her a book printed in Braille. It was much easier for her fingertips to follow the raised dots than it was to follow raised print in ordinary letters.

''Now let's start writing in Braille,'' Teacher spelled into her hand. ''This little frame you've been playing with is called a Braille Slate, and this thing you use to punch the holes is called a Stylus.''

Teacher watched while Helen fitted a piece of paper into the Braille Slate. Then Helen picked up the Stylus and began punching holes, from left to right—as she had learned to write with a pencil. Teacher shook her head and sighed. She sat thinking for several minutes while Helen happily punched away.

Then she gave Helen a thin piece of paper and a pencil. Guiding her hand and pushing the pencil down hard, she had Helen print the word "dog."

When they turned the paper over, Helen could feel the letters, but they were all wrong—backwards, like this: pob.

Next Teacher had Helen punch the word "dog" in Braille in the slate, starting from left to right. And when they took the paper out and turned it over, the Braille letters were wrong, too—backwards.

Teacher then put the paper back into the slate and, guiding her hand, had Helen punch out the word "dog," working from right to left, instead of from left to right as she would with a pencil. And when they took the paper out and turned it over, there was the word "dog," as it should be!

Helen sat absolutely still for a moment, thinking hard. Then she nodded her head, picked up the stylus and punched out some more words, starting from right to left.

Eagerly she pulled the paper out and turned it over. And there the words were under her fingers in dots—not backwards, but the way they should be. A pleased smile lighted up her face as

Teacher patted her shoulder approvingly. Teacher reached for Helen's hand and spelled:

"That's it! Now all you need is to keep doing it until you can do it faster."

Writing in Braille, Helen discovered, was much more fun than writing with a pencil, because she could turn the paper over and read what she had written. She wanted to write all her letters in Braille. It was so much easier.

Teacher gave the matter some thought before she tried to explain why she couldn't. For Helen, so far, had shown no sign that she realized that other people weren't blind, too. She did not yet know eyes were to see with.

Finally, Teacher gently took Helen's hand. Her fingers moved slowly and carefully as they spelled:

"Not everybody, dear, can read Braille, as you do. This is something very special!"

And Helen felt pleased and very proud of herself.

10.

"A Lion Has a Big Purr!"

HELEN WRIGGLED with impatience as Teacher finished tying her hair-ribbon and gave a final expert twist to one of her light brown curls. Eagerly she reached for her hat.

She could hardly wait to be off. For this was a very special occasion. Helen and Teacher were going to the circus.

Teacher smiled but shook her head as she watched Helen's swiftly moving fingers. For they spelled:

"Helen will see a lion!"

Teacher had doubts. "Seeing" for Helen meant "feeling." To "see" a lion, she would have to pass her hands over its great, powerful body.

It was true that Helen had a way with animals. She had no fear of them. And they trusted her, seeming to understand that they must be gentle with her. But it was unlikely that a seven-year-old girl could go inside a cage and stroke a lion!

"Perhaps Helen will see a lion," Teacher spelled into her little pupil's hand. "But a lion is very big and strong and wild. And he may not like little girls. There will be many other things to see."

But that didn't satisfy Helen. Her small fingers spelled back:

"Helen will bring the lion home and make him gentle!"

When Helen had taken her first steps outside her dark and lonely prison, the world she had entered had been, to her, a very small place. It was limited to things she could reach out and touch, with Teacher's fingers spelling their names into her hand. But with each new word she learned, her world had widened out.

From familiar places—the pump house, her home, the fields and woods near by—Helen had begun to range far and wide, through the magic of Teacher's fingers in her hand.

As they sat high up in the branches of their favorite tree, Teacher had told her about strange wild beasts that roamed through forests and jungles on faraway continents. Of all the beasts, Helen was most interested in the lion.

"In the animal world the lion belongs to the cat family," Teacher had told her. And she had explained that this made the lion a distant cousin of her own purring little kitten.

More than any other animal, Helen wanted to see this big cat who was king of the beasts.

For several weeks—from the day the first gay posters had appeared on billboards around town—Teacher had been telling Helen about the circus.

She had told her about the clowns, with funny faces that made people laugh. The tight-rope walkers, balanced on a single wire high above the ground. The trapeze artists, leaping through space from swing to swing.

And of course she had described the jungle beasts. Funny little monkeys that did tricks. Long-necked giraffes. And huge, lumbering elephants that could reach out with their long trunks and take peanuts out of your hand!

"And lions!" Helen would always add.

Now the great day had come at last. Helen clung to Teacher's hand as they walked toward the circus grounds. She could not see the big tent. Nor could she hear the chatter of the crowd, the shouts of the sideshow barkers, or the steam calliope wailing out a circus tune.

But she knew when they had arrived just the same. By the smells!

Sawdust on the ground—she remembered that smell from a visit to a sawmill. She recognized, too, the mouth-watering smell of hot buttered popcorn and hamburgers sizzling on outdoor grills. Teacher had told her these things would be there.

But there was another smell—new, strange. The smell that belongs to the circus. The smell of animals and hay and straw and the disinfectant they put into the water when they clean the cages. All mingled together. Helen's small nose twitched with excitement.

She and Teacher found the monkeys first. Teacher explained to their keeper that Helen could not see or hear.

"Will she be scared if I let them jump up on her?" he asked.

Teacher said no. And the next thing Helen knew, a little creature with tiny hands—just like human hands—was on her shoulder. With delight her fingers found his funny, wrinkled little face and his long tail with a curl in the end.

Helen laughed and so did everybody who was watching them as the monkey grabbed her hat and gravely tried it on his own head. Then one of his little brothers was on her other shoulder, earnestly examining her hair-ribbon.

"I don't know who's having the most fun—
my monkeys or your little girl!" the keeper said.

And he and Teacher both laughed when she
told him what Helen was saying with her fingers:

"Can we take one home? Please, can we?
Please?"

Word got around the circus grounds that a
little girl who was blind and deaf was there,
and everybody set out to give her a good time.

The clowns let her run her fingers over their
funny faces. The trapeze artists lowered one of
their swings and let her swing in it. The acrobats
went slowly through their act, so that Helen
could follow their movements with her hands.

When she and Teacher came to the giraffe
one of the men lifted her up so she could feel
its long neck. A big black bear politely held out
a shaggy paw for her to shake.

Helen was a little startled when she felt the
moist, snuffling end of the elephant's trunk
grab a peanut out of her hand. But she wasn't
frightened.

Then came a big moment. She was introduced
to the Oriental Princess, who rode the elephant
in the circus parade. After Helen had examined
her spangled costume and jeweled headdress,
the Oriental Princess asked Teacher, "Would
the little girl like to take a ride?"

And Helen rode in triumph around the ring, sitting in the lap of the Oriental Princess on the elephant's huge, swaying head.

Finally Teacher led her to the lions' cage. Then Helen's fingers began to fly.

"What is it she wants?" the lion trainer asked.

Teacher sighed.

"She wants to see a lion," she explained. "But the only way she could do it would be to go into the cage and run her hands over one of the lions."

The trainer stroked his chin thoughtfully.

"I never let kids get near my big cats," he said. "Kids jump around too much. And if one of these fellows gets excited, he can do a lot of damage—without meaning to."

He stroked his chin some more. Then he asked, "Has the little girl been around animals much?"

"Oh, yes," Teacher replied. "She's used to them. And they usually love her."

"Well," the trainer said, "I've got one fellow who's young. He hasn't got his full growth yet. He's tame as a kitten. I can trust him. Want to try it?"

He took out his keys and led them around to a cage set back, away from the crowd.

"I'm not working him in the act yet," he said, looking at the young lion proudly. "And

I keep him back here because I don't want anybody to tease him or frighten him."

As Helen and Teacher followed the trainer into the cage, the lion rose lazily and stretched.

"We've got company, Pete," the trainer said. And he scratched the lion around his ears.

Then he took Helen's hand and placed it on Pete's great tawny back. With the trainer's hand guiding her, Helen passed her hand slowly and gently over the powerful body. Then up into the thick, heavy mane. Pete remained quiet, relaxed.

She found his face. And as she stroked his nose, Pete began to make queer, guttural noises in his throat. Helen couldn't hear them, but she could feel the vibration.

Teacher was a little anxious.

"Is he growling?" she asked.

"No, ma'am," the trainer said with a grin. "It's just his way of saying he likes it!"

They were outside the cage again, when Helen smiled and her fingers began to move.

"What's she saying?" the trainer asked.

"She's saying," Teacher laughed, "that a lion has a big purr!"

11.

Most Famous Child in the World

"SHE'S BITING her nails again."

Teacher's voice sounded discouraged. Both she and Mrs. Keller shook their heads as they watched Helen dreamily chipping away her thumbnail with her front teeth.

Helen, of course, did not know they were watching her.

Teacher stiffened in sudden resolution.

"I hate to do this," she said, "but—"

Swiftly she pounced on Helen, soundly boxing her ears. Reaching into her sewing bag, she pulled out a ribbon. Her fingers pounded into Helen's palm:

"See if this will help you to remember not to bite your nails!"

Then with the ribbon she tied Helen's hands together behind her back.

Helen was too surprised to cry. And the punishment lasted only about half an hour. But there were many things Helen wanted to say. And she could not "talk" with her hands tied together.

"I really think the punishment was harder on Teacher than it was on Helen," Mrs. Keller told her husband that evening. "You should have seen her pacing up and down, watching the clock!"

Helen on the whole was a happy, well-behaved eight-year-old. She no longer had tantrums. But she had some of the faults little girls are apt to have. She was lazy sometimes and untidy and forgetful.

Usually, in order to punish her, Teacher sent her to bed. Rarely was Teacher so severe as she had been about the nail-biting. But she had been trying for months to break Helen of the habit.

Since the child had to do all her talking with her fingers, people watched her hands more than they watched the hands of an ordinary child.

"We can't let her have ugly, chewed-up fingertips!" Teacher told Mrs. Keller.

This was all the more important because Helen had become the most famous child in the world. Stories about her had appeared wherever newspapers were printed. In many lands and in many languages people had read about the little girl who could not see or hear or talk, and about all the things she had learned to do.

Helen did not know about these newspaper stories. Nor did she know that she was famous. Teacher did not want her to know.

"If she did, it might ruin her," Teacher told Helen's parents. "We don't want her to become spoiled—a horrid little show-off!"

Since nobody could talk to Helen except with his fingers in her hand, it was not hard to keep things from her. Not many people knew how to use the Manual Alphabet.

It was an eager and excited little Helen who started off on a trip with Teacher one lovely morning in May a few weeks after the nail-biting incident. As the train pulled away from the station at Tuscumbia, she settled herself happily on the plush seat and reached for Teacher's hand.

She knew that Teacher's fingers would tell her all about the things she saw as the train sped through the countryside. The beautiful flowering fruit trees. Men and horses working in the fields. Steeples and rooftops and streets in the towns they passed through. And sometimes, off in the distance, tall mountains wearing white clouds for caps.

Helen had learned about mountains. She and Teacher had built mountain ranges in the sand down by the Tennessee River near home. They had dug river channels, too, and had built dams of pebbles to make lakes. This was the way she learned geography.

Helen loved to ride on trains. And she was thrilled about this trip. Teacher had told her that it was going to be the longest trip she had ever taken. They were going to Boston, away up north in Massachusetts. It would take them two whole days and a night to get there. They would sleep and have their meals on the train!

"Just like living in a house on wheels!" Helen told herself.

In Boston they would stay at the Perkins Institution, where Teacher had gone to school. And Helen would play with the little blind children.

For a long time Helen had not understood the meaning of the word "blind." She had realized that other people talked with their mouths, although she could not. But the knowledge that eyes were to see with came more slowly.

Finally one day her fingers had asked Teacher a question:

"What do my eyes do?"

Teacher thought carefully for a moment before her fingers spelled the answer:

"I see with my eyes. But you see with your fingers."

Helen put her hand up to Teacher's eyes, and

then to her own. She was puzzled. For to her fingertips they felt the same.

While Teacher watched anxiously, Helen's small fingers began to move.

"My eyes are sick," they spelled.

But Helen really did not worry much about her eyes. She had grown used to seeing with her fingers. They served her well.

Now, Helen was looking forward to playing with the blind children because Teacher had told her they could talk to her with their fingers in her hand. Most of her playmates could not.

Teacher told her about Laura Bridgman, who lived at the school. Laura Bridgman could not talk with her mouth either.

"People talk to her, as I talk to you, with their fingers in her hand," Teacher had explained. "And so all the little blind children know how to do it."

When Helen reached the Perkins Institution in Boston she found that she could talk easily with Laura Bridgman too. She spent many happy hours playing with the blind children at Perkins. There were all kinds of toys at the school, made especially for blind children, and books written in Braille.

This was the first of many trips Helen took to Boston while she was growing up. During those visits she met several famous people.

There was a kind, gentle old man who was a poet, named John Greenleaf Whittier. And another famous writer, Oliver Wendell Holmes, who printed a letter she wrote him in his magazine.

There were two famous clergymen. One was Dr. Edward Everett Hale, who wrote *The Man Without a Country*. Dr. Hale said he and Helen were distantly related, and he always called her "Little Cousin." And there was Bishop Phillips Brooks, who held her on his lap and told her about God, while Teacher spelled his words into her hand.

Once while they were on their way to Boston they stopped at Washington to visit Dr. Alexander Graham Bell, the famous inventor of the telephone. He was the same Dr. Bell who had told Mr. and Mrs. Keller where to find a teacher for Helen.

While they were in Washington Dr. Bell took Helen to the White House to see President Cleveland. He was the first President she met. During her lifetime she was to meet every President after Grover Cleveland, including President Eisenhower, who, she said, gave her "a lovely smile."

Helen herself became more and more famous during those childhood years. Many people sent her gifts and wrote letters to her. In Maine a ship was named after her. And in faraway London Queen Victoria asked a visiting American about her.

But to Helen, who didn't know she was famous, these were all just nice people, who liked little girls. And because she was unspoiled, friendly, and happy, they all loved her.

Helen's first visit to Boston was the most exciting, because it was the first time she had been so far away from home. She liked being at Perkins Institution, but when summer came, bringing hot weather, she was glad when Teacher told her they were going on a vacation at the seashore. They went to Cape Cod, not far from Boston. Helen wanted to "see" the ocean and play in the waves.

The first afternoon she could hardly wait to get into her pretty new bathing suit. Without any thought of fear, she raced out across the warm sand into the cool water.

At first it was wonderful. She loved the way the billows lifted her like mighty arms. But suddenly a great big wave came rolling in, and she was helpless as it tossed her about and dumped her head-over-heels onto the sand. She was breathless and panicky until she felt Teacher's comforting arms about her.

It took a moment to get the water and sand out

of her mouth and ears. Then her fingers began to fly.

"Who put salt in the water?" she demanded.

Teacher had neglected to tell her that ocean water is salty!

Although Helen had been frightened, this did not keep her out of the ocean. She soon learned to handle herself in the surf and loved to sit on a big rock, with the salty spray washing over her.

There were smooth, quiet pools to play in, too. And before the summer was over, she wrote to her cousin back home:

"I can float now."

12.

Winter in the Snow

HELEN and Teacher were back in Boston the following winter, staying at the Perkins Institution.

It was Helen's first winter in the north. And it was great fun for a nine-year-old who had never played in the snow before.

They had arrived in Boston in the autumn, and Helen was surprised to find that it was so much colder than Alabama. But she loved to go scuffing through the dried leaves in the park. And Teacher's fingers told her:

"The trees are all bare and black. But their branches make a lovely pattern, like lace, against the sky."

Among the new friends they had made in the north were the Chamberlins, a delightful family, who lived on a place called Red Farm, near the village of Wrentham, about twenty-five miles from Boston. Mr. Chamberlin wrote articles for the *Transcript*, an old and highly respected Boston newspaper.

Several times that winter Helen and Teacher were invited to visit the Chamberlins and their children at Red Farm. This was a jolly place, with many dogs and horses. The Chamberlin house was big and rambling. It overlooked King Philip's Pond, named after a famous old Indian warrior, of the days of the Pilgrims.

Helen, all bundled up and wearing her new overshoes, was playing outdoors with the other children on the day it first began to snow. Teacher pulled off one of Helen's mittens and let some of the first big, fluffy flakes drift down into her hand.

"Where did they go?" Helen's fingers spelled anxiously. For of course they melted as soon as they touched her warm skin.

All that afternoon the snow came down and that night a great wind came howling out of the northeast. Helen could feel the vibrations as the house groaned and creaked and the branches of the big trees lashed about.

But inside the house everyone was warm and snug and merry, popping corn in front of a great open fire. The Chamberlins sang songs and told stories, which Teacher spelled into Helen's hand.

When they went out the next morning the sun was shining on a world made of snow.

Before long Helen's red mittens were wet and soggy as she joined the other children making snowballs and building a snow man.

In the afternoon Mr. Chamberlin brought out a long, sleek toboggan.

"Do you think Helen will be frightened if we give her a ride on it?" he asked.

"No, of course not!" Teacher replied.

They loaded the toboggan—as many as could get on—poised on the crest of a steep bank above King Philip's Pond. The pond was frozen solid, from shore to shore.

Teacher showed Helen where to hold on. Then she spelled into her hand:

"We'll be going very fast. So hold on tight. I'm right here behind you. Lean back against me, and when you feel me swaying you do the same. This is going to be fun!"

When everyone was ready, Mr. Chamberlin called out, "Let's go!" One of the boys gave them a shove, and they were off.

For an instant Helen felt as though all the breath in her body was being blown out, as the toboggan took a great leap down the bank.

They plunged through a snowdrift, leaped

across some hollows, and swooped down upon
the ice. Flying snow stung Helen's cheeks as
they shot across the frozen pond. It was wild,
mad, wonderful! Like flying!

They were away over on the other side of
the pond when they finally slowed down and
stopped. Laughing and shouting, they tumbled
off the toboggan and shook off the snow.

"Is Helen all right?" Mr. Chamberlin called
out.

"She is!" Teacher assured him. Then she
laughed. For Helen had jerked off one of her
mittens, and her half-frozen fingers fluttered
like little red birds as they spelled:

"Let's do it again!"

For the rest of the visit, Helen and the other
children spent every moment they could outdoors in the snow. One day a team of horses was
hitched to a bob sleigh, filled with hay and big,
shaggy robes made of buffalo hide. And Helen
had her first sleigh ride.

The winter wasn't all playtime, however.
Presently she and Teacher were back in Boston
at the Perkins School. Helen did not go to
classes with the other children. But she had lessons every day, with Teacher.

Helen was studying English grammar, geography, American history and arithmetic, now.
She liked arithmetic and was very good at it.

This was remarkable, because, being blind, she could not write the figures down and multiply, add, subtract, or divide them with a pencil, but had to carry them all in her head!

"I don't know myself how she does it!" Teacher remarked to one of the other teachers at the Perkins School. "She has a wonderful memory!"

Helen loved the library at the Perkins School, where there were shelves filled with books printed in Braille. She spent many happy hours there, running her fingertips along the rows of raised dots. Some of the books she read were for children. But others were books for grownups. In these there were many words she did not understand. But that did not bother her. She simply skipped over them and managed to get a general idea of what the book was about!

When February came, and the days began to grow longer, Helen looked forward eagerly to the summer, when she and Teacher would be going back home to Alabama.

She wanted to be with her parents and her little sister, Mildred. But she was just as anxious to see her beautiful new mastiff puppy.

A friend had sent the puppy to her home in Tuscumbia not long before Christmas, and Mrs. Keller, who had learned Braille so she could write to her little girl, had written Helen about it.

Helen called the puppy Lioness.

"I hope Lioness is still a puppy when I get home in the summer," Helen told Teacher. "Lioness is going to be a big dog, but I hope she won't be all grown up before I see her!"

As her fingers spelled these words to Teacher, Helen thought of another hope she had had for many months. She had come a long, long way out of her dark and lonely prison. But there was something else she wished for. Something she wanted to learn to do. She wished for it more than she wished for anything else in the world.

Although it seemed impossible that her wish would ever be granted, it came true that spring in a way she had not expected at all.

13.

"I Am Not Dumb Now!"

It was late March, and Helen was thinking more and more about going home for the summer, when she and Teacher heard about Ragnhild Kaata.

Ragnhild was a Norwegian child, blind and deaf like Helen, and she had learned to do what nobody thought a blind-deaf child could do. Ragnhild had learned to talk like other people.

Helen was so excited at this news that her fingers almost ran the words together in a blur as they spelled:

"If a little girl in Norway can do it, I can do it, too!"

This was the thing Helen had wanted so much to do—more than anything else in the world.

As a very little girl, before Teacher came,

Helen had often felt her parents' lips move as they talked to each other. She had thought then that they were playing a game they wouldn't play with her. This had made her feel left out, hurt and angry.

But she had known for some time now that they had not been playing a game. They had been talking. And she had found out, too, that most people hear with their ears.

Helen could not see how people's lips looked when they moved to form words. Nor could she hear any voices, not even her own. Since there had been no way for her to learn to use her voice, she was dumb. She could "talk" only with her fingers.

The hardest thing about being dumb was that most people could not understand her, because they did not know the Manual Alphabet. And Helen had so many things she wanted to say! Even with Teacher it was hard, because her thoughts would race away ahead of her fingers.

"Slow down!" Teacher would spell into her hand. "Your fingers are wiggling so fast that they don't make sense!"

Helen now knew where voices came from. If she placed her hand against Teacher's throat, she could feel the vibration.

She had also learned that words are pronounced with the mouth and lips. For she had learned to "read" Teacher's lips by placing her fingers on them.

For a person who can see, lip-reading is not very difficult. But for a person who is blind it is almost impossible. Helen, however, had learned it. And that had made her all the more determined to learn to talk with her throat and lips.

For some time now she had been struggling to speak. But the sounds she made were very unpleasant. Often Teacher would sadly shake her head and try to get her interested in something else.

Still Helen would not give up.

"I know I can make sounds in my throat," her fingers spelled to Teacher. "I can feel them. So why can't I make talking sounds?"

"Sometimes people born deaf do learn to speak," Teacher said slowly, with Helen's fingers on her lips. "But their voices are usually dull and flat and unpleasant. That's because they can't hear themselves.

"Learning to talk would be even harder for you because you can't see how people use their lips and tongues and the muscles in their faces."

"But I can *feel* them," Helen's stubborn little fingers spelled back.

Now that she had heard about the little girl in Norway, she was more determined than ever to learn to speak. So Teacher decided to take her to see Miss Fuller, who was the principle of a school for deaf and dumb children in Boston. Helen fairly danced with excitement as they walked into Miss Fuller's office.

If Teacher had any doubts whether Miss Fuller could teach Helen to talk, Helen had none.

"I'd like to help her," Miss Fuller said, watching Helen's earnest, confident expression. "I'll be glad to give her some lessons. Let's see what she can do."

She let Helen read her lips and told her:

"I shall make different motions with my lips and tongue. Try to make each of these motions with your lips and tongue as you let the sound come out of your throat. We'll start with the *M* sound. It's made this way, with the lips pressed together. Try it."

After several tries, Helen succeeded fairly well. Next they tried the *T* sound, with the tongue touching the front teeth. In an hour Helen learned how to make six sounds—*M*, *T*, *P*, *A*, *S*, and *I*.

Her greatest difficulty was with sounds that are made far back in the mouth. *K*, for instance. And the hard *G*, as in "girl." And she had a lot of trouble with *R* and *L*.

From the very first lesson Helen tried to pronounce words, although neither Miss Fuller nor Teacher could understand them.

"Have patience," Miss Fuller told her. "Learn to make these sounds first, and the words will come later. Now let's try that *K* sound again."

But Helen could not be patient. The words were there, in her throat, struggling to get out, like little birds beating their wings against the bars of a cage. From the moment she was awake in the morning until she went to sleep at night she kept trying—trying—trying.

Teacher's mouth was soon sore from Helen's prodding little fingers, trying to find out how she curled her tongue to make the *L* sound different from the *R* sound. And how she made the *B* sound and the *P* sound.

Miss Fuller was delighted with the progress Helen was making.

"Never before have I had a pupil so eager to learn," she told Teacher.

Finally the day came for Helen's last lesson. She had made a plan for this last lesson, and she had been working on it for days when she was alone.

First she and Miss Fuller went through the letter sounds. Next Helen spoke some of the words she had been learning to pronounce.

"Very, very good," Miss Fuller said, with Helen's fingertips on her lips. "Now the thing you need is practice."

Then Helen tried her plan.

She took a deep breath, her heart pounding with excitement, her whole body straining with the effort she was making.

Slowly, carefully she brought the words out:
"I—am—not—dumb—now!"

The voice was flat, the words not very distinct. She had not yet learned that in some words not all letters are pronounced. So she said "dum-b," pronouncing the silent *B*.

Probably nobody but Miss Fuller and Teacher could have understood what she was saying.

But no cry more triumphant ever rose from any human throat.

14.

Little Tommy Stringer

IT WAS a mild spring day. Helen and Teacher
were sitting in the little room that had been
given them to use as a study at the Perkins
School in Boston. They had just finished an
hour of practicing to improve Helen's speech.

Since Helen did not go to classes with the
other children—who were blind, but not deaf,
too, as she was—she had her lessons alone with
Teacher.

Helen would be eleven years old in a few
weeks now, and she was growing tall and slender. Although it was a year since she had learned
to talk, her speech was still far from perfect.
She and Teacher worked on it every day, trying
new words, over and over again.

Helen no longer talked with her fingers. Although she could not speak clearly, she insisted on trying. When she spoke to strangers, however, Teacher had to repeat the words.

Now Teacher spelled into her hand, "I think we've done enough for today."

As they stood up and stretched, Teacher reached for Helen's hand again.

"I have a sad story to tell you," her fingers spelled. "It's about a little boy named Tommy Stringer."

A letter about Tommy had arrived at the school that morning. Tommy was five years old. A year before, an illness had left him blind and deaf, like Helen. His mother was dead, and his father was unable to take care of him. So Tommy had been sent to a poorhouse near Pittsburgh, Pennsylvania.

Teacher was worried about Tommy. For she thought the poorhouse in Pennsylvania was probably no better than the one in Massachusetts where she had spent four terrible years when she was a child. She had never told Helen about those years. And she did not tell her now.

One thing Helen did know, however. Tommy needed help, just as she had before Teacher came.

"Can't we bring him here and find a teacher for him?" she asked.

"I'm afraid there's no money for that," Teacher's fingers told her.

"Well, let's get some," Helen urged. "I'll write to all my friends and ask them for money to help Tommy."

Writing letters was easy for Helen now, because she had a typewriter. She had learned to use the "touch system," as professional typists do. So the fact that she could not see the keys did not matter. She even wrote most of Teacher's letters for her, because Teacher's eyes were no better, even after another operation.

As she sat down at her typewriter, Helen thought how much luckier she was than poor little Tommy Stringer. Not only did she have Teacher always beside her, but in a few weeks she would be going home for another wonderful summer in Alabama.

She would play again with her little sister, Mildred, whom she loved dearly, and with Lioness and all her other pets.

There was her little donkey, called Neddy. Helen had had a lot of fun the summer before, hitching Neddy to his cart and taking Mildred for rides.

"We'll do it again this summer, many times," she thought happily.

And there was her pony, a black pony with a white star on his forehead. She had named the pony Black Beauty, after the horse in the story which is still read and loved by children today.

Black Beauty was well trained and trustworthy. He knew the paths through the woods so well that he could always find the way home. So Teacher would sometimes unsnap the leading rein, and Helen and Black Beauty would go off by themselves.

Helen loved her pony. But of all her pets she loved Lioness most. She asked about her and sent messages to her in every letter she wrote to her family at home.

"But I mustn't think about Lioness now," she told herself. "I must write some letters about Tommy Stringer."

She put a sheet of paper into her typewriter and was all ready to begin when Teacher brought her a letter, which had just come from her mother. Helen started eagerly to read it. But her fingers had passed over only a few lines of her mother's Braille writing, when she started to cry.

Tears ran down her cheeks as she handed the letter to Teacher. As Teacher read the letter, there were tears in her eyes, too. For Mrs. Keller had written about Lioness, and had sent Helen bad news.

Lioness, a gentle dog, had grown almost as big as a lion, with a deep, loud bark that frightened many people. Unfortunately, she had discovered that it was great fun to chase horses and carriages and to bark at them.

At last a policeman had caught her at it. Not realizing that Lioness was only playing, he had shot her. This was the sad news which Mrs. Keller had had to send to Helen.

It was hard for Helen to realize that Lioness was dead. Although she tried to control herself she was soon sobbing on Teacher's comforting shoulder. Finally, Teacher gently took Helen's hand:

"I think, dear," her fingers spelled, "it may help a little if you go on writing the letters about Tommy. Remember—he, too, must be very lonely and unhappy."

Helen nodded and borrowed Teacher's handkerchief to dry her eyes, since her own was all wet and soggy. And after a few moments, she went back to her typewriter.

During the next few days she wrote several letters. One was about Lioness and was written to the friend who had given her the dog. In it, Helen said, "if the policeman had only known what a good dog she was, he wouldn't have shot her."

Because Helen was a famous child, stories about Lioness were printed in all the newspapers. Before long she began getting letters from people offering to help her find another dog.

These letters came from all over the United States. There were even some from England. Some of them contained money. Some of the writers offered to buy her another dog.

The letters were generous and comforting, but they couldn't bring Lioness back. And Helen and Teacher did not know what to do with the money.

"Why don't we take all that money and put it into a fund to help Tommy Stringer?" Helen asked one morning.

"It would be a wonderful thing to do," Teacher agreed. "But the people who sent it to you wanted you to use it to buy another dog. They might not like it if you used it for something else."

"I'll write to them and ask them if they mind," Helen said. "I'll ask all the people who want to buy a dog for me to give the money to Tommy instead."

For several days Helen was very busy writing letters. And before very long she had enough money to bring Tommy to Boston and to pay his teacher.

Tommy was a bright, attractive little boy, but he never advanced as far as Helen did. Probably because he was not so eager to learn as Helen was. He did learn to use the Manual Alphabet, however. And he was able to earn his living when he grew up, making boxes.

Helen's eagerness to learn was now presenting a problem to Teacher. Teacher had gone only through the sixth grade in school. Helen had already gone beyond the sixth grade in some of her studies.

She had begun to learn French all by herself after finding some French books in Braille in the Perkins School library. And she wanted to learn Latin and Greek, because she and Teacher had read so many stories about the Greek and Roman gods and goddesses that they seemed like real people to her.

"Helen will soon need someone to help her with her studies who has had more education than I have had," Teacher told Mrs. Keller when she and Helen reached home that summer.

"You wouldn't turn her over to someone else and leave her, would you?" Mrs. Keller asked anxiously.

"No, of course not," Teacher replied. "But I think it would be good for her to go to school with other children."

"How could she?" Mrs. Keller asked. "She wouldn't be able to hear what the teacher was saying or see what was written on the blackboard."

"I'd have to go with her, of course," Teacher said, "and spell everything into her hand. She could do her homework on her typewriter. And I believe she could recite in class. She'd try it anyway. She refuses to talk with her fingers any more. At first the teachers would have trouble understanding her. But that would pass, as they got to know her better."

"Well, we don't have to make the decision right away," Mrs. Keller said.

Teacher nodded. "There's plenty of time," she agreed, "but I'll keep looking around for a school." Then with a little sigh she left the vine-covered veranda where they had been sitting and went indoors. There was one problem which she had not mentioned. That was her own eye trouble.

If Helen did go to school, she would need many more school books, as she reached the higher grades. Few of them were printed in Braille. This would mean that her homework would be as much of a job for Teacher as it was for Helen. For Teacher would have to read the books and spell them into her hand.

Although Helen knew that Teacher's eyes were bad, she had no idea how bad they were.

"And I shall try to keep the truth from her," Teacher thought, "just as long as I possibly can."

15.

"I Am Going to Harvard"

THAT FALL Helen and Teacher spent a few weeks
in Boston. While they were there they went one
day to see some friends at Wellesley, a famous
women's college, which is near Boston.

Helen was very much interested when Teacher told her about Wellesley, explaining that it
was a college for women only. As they walked
about the campus, Teacher's fingers in her hand
described the buildings to her and the girls walking by in small groups on their way to classes.

Later, while Teacher and Helen were visiting
with their friends, Helen surprised everybody
by announcing:

"Some day I shall go to college—but I shall
go to Harvard."

Everybody who spends any time in Boston,

as Helen had, knows about Harvard University, in nearby Cambridge. Boston people are very proud of Harvard.

One of Helen's friends wanted to know why she did not want to go to Wellesley. And when Teacher spelled the question into her hand, Helen replied:

"Because there are only girls here."

Everybody laughed, and the subject was dropped for the time being. Nobody took Helen's announcement very seriously. It seemed impossible that a girl who was blind and deaf could go to college.

But when Teacher and Helen were riding back to Boston on the trolley car, Teacher took Helen's hand and spelled into it:

"Where did you ever get the idea you were going to Harvard, dear? Harvard is a men's college. But there is a women's college called Radcliffe which is connected with Harvard. The girls go to classes at Harvard and have the same professors as the men."

"Then that's where I'm going," Helen said.

Teacher smiled and changed the subject.

"She's only eleven," she thought. "She'll forget about it by the time she's old enough for college. But I must find a school, where she can learn more than I can teach her."

Finding a school for Helen, who could neither

see nor hear, was not easy. It took Teacher three years. Finally she decided that Helen should go to the Wright-Humason School, a special school for deaf and dumb children in New York City.

"Although the children there are deaf and dumb, they are not blind," Teacher told Mrs. Keller. "But I feel sure Helen can keep up with them. And I think the teachers there may be able to improve her speech. They will let me go to classes with her, so I can spell everything into her hand."

Helen was fourteen when she entered the Wright-Humason School in New York. As Teacher had expected, she did very well indeed in her school work, although her speech did not improve as much as Teacher had hoped it would.

When she had been at the Wright-Humason School for nearly two years, Teacher decided she had better have a serious talk with her about college. For Helen had firmly decided that she wanted to go to college, and kept insisting that she was going to Radcliffe.

Teacher thought the matter over carefully before she discussed it with Helen. She had always believed in treating Helen exactly like any other child. She hated to discourage her in anything she wanted to do. But she believed that Helen must be made to realize that it would be difficult for a girl who could not see or hear to go to college. Her fingers spelled the words slowly and carefully into Helen's hand:

"First of all, you must understand that no allowances would be made for you in college because you are blind and deaf. You would have to keep up with your studies just like everybody else. You would have to work much harder—probably twice as hard."

Helen jerked her hand away impatiently.

"I can work twice as hard as anybody else," she said. "I'm very strong."

Teacher gently took her hand again.

"I know, dear. But you would be up against something you've never been up against before. All the other girls would be able to see and hear. I know—the students here are not blind. But they are deaf, as you are. If they could both see and hear, you'd have a harder time keeping up with them."

"Then I ought to go to school with students who can see and hear," Helen said.

Again Teacher's fingers moved in her hand:

"Another thing—they tell me Radcliffe is one of the toughest women's colleges in the country to get into. They might not want you."

"Anyway, I'll try," Helen said.

Since Helen, being blind, could not handle money, she had never yet thought much about

it. She had no idea that it would cost a lot of
money to go through college. But Teacher
thought about it, a good deal.

Helen's father was not a rich man. As editor
of a small weekly newspaper in Alabama, he had
never made much money. For several years he
had not even paid Teacher's salary, although
Helen did not know this. A generous friend had
made it possible for Helen to go to the Wright-
Humason School in New York.

In New York, Helen had made many new
friends, some of whom were very rich. Some of
them were not so rich, but were famous. One of
these was Mark Twain, whose stories about Tom
Sawyer and Huck Finn she had read and loved.
When word got around among her New York
friends that Helen wanted to go to college, but
that the Kellers could not afford to send her,
Mark Twain said, "Well, why don't we do something about it?" So they got together and raised
the money which would be needed.

But before she could enter any college, Helen
would have to pass some examinations. The entrance examinations for Radcliffe were the same
as for Harvard—very difficult. Teacher thought
Helen should go to a good school which would
prepare her for these examinations. There were,
of course, no such schools for girls who were

blind and deaf. Nobody who was blind and deaf had ever tried to go to a prep school or to college before.

Teacher talked the problem over with Helen's friends who were planning to pay for her education. Some were doubtful about how well Helen would do in a school where all the other students could see and hear.

"But that's what she'll be up against when she goes to college," Teacher said. "She might as well try it now. Let's give her a chance."

After looking over several schools, Teacher decided on the Cambridge School for Young Ladies. This was a preparatory school for girls who planned to go to Radcliffe. It was in Cambridge, just outside Boston, and was near the college.

One bright October morning in 1896, the girls in Frau Grote's German class at the Cambridge School for Young Ladies looked up with interest when a tall, slender girl with wavy light-brown hair walked into the classroom.

A fashionably dressed, attractive young woman was with her. Now and then, she would lightly touch the girl's arm, seeming to guide her as they moved along.

The girl was not clumsy, though. She walked easily, with a kind of grace. Her eyes were blue.

Only if you looked at her intently did you notice that they always stared straight ahead.

Helen Keller and Teacher had entered their first class in a school where Helen was the only pupil who was both blind and deaf.

All the girls had been told about Helen.

"The only way she can find out about what is going on is for someone to spell it out in her hand," Mr. Gilman, the principal, had explained. "That is why her teacher, Miss Sullivan, will come to classes with her. You will notice that Miss Sullivan holds Helen's hand most of the time. When she does it, she will be spelling words into her hand."

Mr. Gilman had also told his students how Helen had learned to talk.

"She will recite in class, like everybody else," he had said. "At first her voice will sound odd to you. And it may be hard to understand her. But as you get to know her better, it will be easier for you."

The teachers, too, had been told about Helen. None of them had ever had a pupil before who was blind and deaf. After Helen entered the school Mr. Gilman and Frau Grote learned to use the Manual Alphabet. But Frau Grote did not know how to spell English words very well, and sometimes the whole class would laugh—including Helen, Teacher, and Frau Grote herself—when she and Helen would get mixed up.

The students at the Cambridge School lived in small houses near the school. Teacher and Helen lived with several of the girls in a beautiful house that had once belonged to William Dean Howells, a famous author whom Helen had met in New York.

The girls liked Helen, even though at first none of them could talk to her. Some of them did learn the Manual Alphabet, but their efforts to spell words into Helen's hand were often clumsy. Helen would laugh with them at their mistakes, and she could usually guess at what they were trying to say. She played games with them—even Blind Man's Buff—and sometimes she went on long hikes with them.

With Helen, however, her studies always had to come first, and they did not leave her much time for play. Teacher had been right when she warned Helen that she might have to work twice as hard as the other girls.

There was a great deal of homework, and this was even harder on Teacher than it was on Helen. There were so many books to be read, and so few of them were printed in Braille! Sometimes Teacher wondered if her tired, aching eyes would get her through another day. But she said nothing about it to anyone. And somehow she managed to read the books Helen needed and to spell them into her hand.

Helen did remarkably well her first year at the school. But when she started her second year, her work did not go so well. It was impossible to get books in Braille that would help her in mathematics, and as a result she began to fall behind. At last it was decided that she should leave the school and study with a tutor, a young man named Merton S. Keith.

Helen would have been bitterly disappointed at having to leave the school if the Chamberlins had not invited her and Teacher to come and stay with them at Red Farm, in Wrentham, where they had spent many happy week ends and vacations. Wrentham is near Boston, and Mr. Keith was able to go back and forth on a trolley car.

The work with Mr. Keith went very well, and at the end of a year and a half Helen was ready to take her final college entrance examinations.

The examinations went on for several days, and Helen worried about them a great deal. Teacher was not allowed to sit in the room with her, and a young man from the Perkins School, who knew the Manual Alphabet, sat beside her to spell the questions into her hand. Helen wrote the answers on her typewriter.

At last the ordeal was over, and Helen and

Teacher went back to Red Farm, where word came before long that Helen had passed in everything.

She was now ready to enter Radcliffe College.

16.

A Dream Comes True

HELEN WAS ready for Radcliffe, but now she faced a new problem. The professors at Radcliffe made it quite plain that they did not want her. They simply could not believe that a girl who was both blind and deaf could go through college. They suggested that she take a few easy subjects, without trying for a diploma.

Other colleges heard about how Helen was trying to enter Radcliffe and how she was not wanted there. Two of these colleges—Cornell University and the University of Chicago—invited her to come to them. But Helen thanked them and said no.

"If I went to either of those colleges," she told Teacher, "they might make it too easy for me. *I am going to Radcliffe.*"

Weeks went by, while Helen and Teacher waited at Red Farm hoping for word that Helen would be allowed to enter Radcliffe. But no word came. Finally Helen sat down at her typewriter and wrote a letter to the chairman of the committee of professors that would decide whether she could enter the college. She ended the letter with these words:

"I realize that the obstacles in the way of my receiving a college education are very great. But a true soldier does not admit defeat before the battle."

No college could turn away a student with that spirit. Helen Keller entered Radcliffe that fall.

A day or two after the college opened, the Freshman class met to elect officers. To her surprise, Helen was asked to make a speech and was elected vice-president of the Freshman class.

"I didn't think most of the girls would even know I was alive!" she told Teacher.

This was funny, for many newspapers had printed stories about Helen Keller, the first blind and deaf person ever to go to college. But Helen was seldom told of these stories, and the few she heard about she did not take very seriously.

Helen and Teacher found a charming little house in Cambridge, where they lived with an Irish maid named Bridget to look after them.

All young people loved Teacher, for she was gay and witty. Whenever she and Helen were not too busy working, their little house was filled with company.

But for Helen there was less time for fun than there was for the other girls at Radcliffe. She read Braille pages until the tips of her fingers bled from rubbing them across the rough, raised dots. And the books she could not get in Braille Teacher had to read to her. Often far into the night—long after her classmates who had been out having a good time were home and in bed—Helen and Teacher toiled on. Teacher would hold the book close to her failing eyes, her fingers moving swiftly in Helen's palm.

Helen now knew how bad Teacher's eyes were. The strain on them had been very great while Helen was in prep school. Now it was much, much worse. Books—books—books—always more books to be read. At times Helen was in despair when she thought of all the books and of Teacher's overworked eyes.

"Don't you think I'd better read that to you again?" Teacher's fingers would ask. "I don't think you understood it all."

"Oh, yes, I did," Helen would assure her. But she hadn't understood it all. And sometimes she would fall behind in her work.

She tried again and again to get Teacher to

go to the eye doctor. But Teacher always put it off.

"Are you afraid of what he'll tell you?" Helen would ask.

"No, of course not!" Teacher's fingers would tell her. "Don't be silly!"

Finally one day Teacher had to stop reading right in the middle of a sentence. Then, at last, she went to her eye doctor. Helen went with her.

"How many hours a day have you been reading to Helen?" the doctor asked.

When Teacher admitted that sometimes it was as much as five hours a day, he was horrified.

"Miss Sullivan, this is sheer madness!" he exclaimed. "You must stop it, if you want to save what little eyesight you have left."

"What did the doctor say?" Helen demanded as she and Teacher left his office.

"He said I should rest my eyes a little more," Teacher spelled into her hand.

Although Teacher had not told her what the doctor really said, Helen knew the trouble was serious. In fact, she had known it ever since the day Teacher had had to stop reading in the middle of a sentence. And now she felt guilty every time Teacher read to her.

Helen became so worried and discouraged that she was almost ready to leave college. But finally a young woman was found who knew the

Manual Alphabet and could read the books and spell them into Helen's hand.

In spite of the hard work and her worries, Helen enjoyed her studies, especially English. Her English professor was Charles Copeland.

At first Helen did not do very well in English. Professor Copeland thought it was because she was trying to write compositions just like those the other students wrote. This meant that she was writing of things she knew nothing about, since she could not see or hear as the others did. Finally, one day, Professor Copeland had a talk with her, Teacher spelling his words into her hand.

"Why don't you try to write about things you know about?" he asked Helen. "Think back to the things that have happened in your own life. Write about those things."

Helen tried his plan, and Professor Copeland was so pleased with her compositions that he showed them to some of his friends. One day the editor of a magazine called *The Ladies' Home Journal* came to Cambridge to see Helen and Teacher.

"I have read some of Miss Keller's compositions," he told them. "We'd like to print them in our magazine." Then he offered to pay for them a sum of money that left Helen and Teacher a little breathless.

About the same time, a book publisher in New York offered to put the compositions into a book after they had been printed in the magazine. He said, however, that they would have to be made longer, and more would have to be written.

Helen and Teacher agreed to do the writing without realizing how much work it would be. When this was added to Helen's college work, it was too much for them. They were in real trouble.

Then, one day a friend brought a young Harvard instructor named John Macy to see them. Mr. Macy learned the Manual Alphabet quickly, so that he could talk to Helen. And with his help she finished the book. It was called *The Story of My Life,* and in it she wrote about her childhood and how Teacher had led her out of her dark and lonely prison.

The Story of My Life was published while Helen was a Junior at Radcliffe. It was printed in many languages, and in Braille. It has been read by people all over the world and still may be found in many school libraries.

Helen still had one more year of college. But with the young woman and John Macy to help with the reading, it was easier.

Finally, on a lovely June day in 1904, ninety-six young women in caps and gowns received their diplomas from Radcliffe College. Because

Radcliffe was connected with Harvard, the diplomas were signed by the President of Harvard University.

The graduate whom everybody noticed was a tall, serious young woman named Helen Adams Keller, graduated *cum laude*—with honor. Teacher was proud, but not completely satisfied. She had hoped it would be *summa cum laude*—with highest honor. She felt that it was her fault that it wasn't.

That day there were stories about Helen in many newspapers, because she was the first blind and deaf person ever to earn a college diploma.

One of the stories mentioned "a little woman in black" who sat beside Helen among the graduates.

That was Teacher.

mark. They had been asked by the United States
Government to go as good-will ambassadors
from the American people.

It was not the longest trip they had ever taken

17.

"I Must Earn My Living"

As soon as the graduation exercises were over,
Helen said good-by to her classmates and the
professors. Proudly carrying her new diploma,
she set out with Teacher for an hour's ride on
the trolley car to their new home.

With some money a friend had given them,
Helen and Teacher had bought an abandoned
farm near Wrentham, where they had spent so
many happy times with the Chamberlins at Red
Farm.

Carpenters, plumbers, electricians, and paint-
ers had been at work on the old farmhouse and
had made it into a very beautiful house.

While Helen and Teacher had been at the
graduation exercises, moving men had taken
the last load of furniture out to the new home.

Bridget, their maid, had gone out to get the place settled for them. They were looking forward eagerly to their first night there. Leaving the trolley car at Wrentham, they set out on foot for their new home.

Soon Teacher could see the big white house, surrounded by a smooth green lawn, with here and there some fine old trees, and the lawn sloping gently down to a lake.

As they approached the house, an enormous dog came bounding out to meet them. It was Thora, Helen's Great Dane. In her enthusiasm Thora almost knocked Teacher down. But she had been trained never to jump on Helen, no matter how glad she was to see her.

Thora followed them as they walked down to the lake. In the boathouse they found Helen's canoe and her rowboat. The oars were equipped with leather bands so they could not slip out of the oarlocks.

Helen had learned to paddle bow in the canoe, with someone paddling stern to guide it. Usually, when she rowed her boat, someone in the stern would steer it with a rudder. But sometimes, when the lake was smooth, she could row by herself, steering by the scent of the water grasses and lilies and the bushes along the shore.

"Is the diving board up?" Helen asked as

they walked out onto the dock. Teacher told her it was.

As a little girl, Helen had learned to swim and dive in King Philip's Pond, at Red Farm. She could even swim under water.

"Your rope is up, too," Teacher's fingers told her.

Dangling from a tree was a very long rope. When Helen went swimming by herself she would tie the rope around her waist, and it would guide her back to the shore.

The farm, long neglected, had grown up in woods. And now Teacher told Helen about the paths the workmen had cut through the woods. They had stretched wires from tree to tree along the paths, to guide her when she went for a walk alone.

"Let's see if our bicycle is here," Helen said.

They found it waiting for them in the barn. It was a tandem bicycle, with two seats. They loved to ride it along quiet country roads, Teacher on the front seat to steer it, and Helen pedaling happily along on the rear seat.

Leaving the barn, they went into the house and settled down in their lovely home for the happiest days of their lives. It was a gay household, with many guests.

From Mrs. Keller and from Martha Washington's mother back in Alabama, Teacher had learned to make some famous southern dishes. She liked to cook for her friends. She had also learned from Mrs. Keller a lot about raising flowers. Now at Wrentham she spent many happy hours working in her garden.

The friend who came most often to the big white house was John Macy, the Harvard instructor who had helped Helen at Radcliffe. For John had fallen in love with Teacher. But for a whole year Teacher kept changing her mind.

On the day when she finally said yes, Teacher found Helen and John Macy doubled up with laughter.

"I was telling Helen," John explained, "that I hoped you wouldn't change your mind again. But, to play it safe, I thought we'd better print on the wedding invitations, 'Subject to change without notice.' "

After the wedding, Helen and John Macy settled down to serious writing. He wrote articles and books. He also was able to help Helen, which took the strain off Teacher's eyes.

Helen had expected to earn her living by writing. But now she was having very little success with it. She was especially discouraged because nobody wanted to read an article she had written on how to take care of babies' eyes so that the babies would not go blind.

"The trouble is that nobody wants to read

anything unless I write about myself," she told Teacher and John Macy at the breakfast table one morning. "And I've written everything I can about myself!"

John nodded sympathetically. "I'm afraid it will always be that way," he spelled into her hand. "And there is, of course, a limit to what you can write about yourself!"

Later that morning Helen was sitting at her typewriter, trying to think of something to write, when Teacher came in with the mail. There was a letter for Helen. Teacher opened it and reached for Helen's hand.

"It's from Andrew Carnegie!" Teacher's fingers spelled.

Andrew Carnegie was then one of the richest men in the world, having made his fortune in the steel business. His money helped to build many libraries all over the United States.

Teacher's fingers moved swiftly in Helen's hand. Mr. Carnegie wanted to help Helen and was offering her a pension, a regular income for the rest of her life.

"It's wonderful of him," Helen said. "But I don't want a pension. I must *earn* my living as other people do."

So later that day she wrote a letter to Mr. Carnegie, thanked him for his generous offer —and refused politely to accept his help.

But how was she to earn her living if she could not do it by writing? This was the question Helen kept turning over and over in her mind.

She said little about it to Teacher or John Macy, however. It was her problem—to figure out for herself. Teacher did not interfere.

"But we'll have to think of some way to earn money before long," Teacher told John. "There's still some of Helen's college money left, but it won't last forever."

One day a letter came from someone at the Pond Lecture Bureau with an offer to Helen to go on a paid lecture tour.

"Me—on a lecture tour?" Helen said when Teacher read the letter to her. "I could never give lectures."

"Let's think about it," Teacher's fingers spelled in her hand. "Maybe you could."

Helen did think about it—a great deal. If she accepted the offer and did go on a lecture trip, it would be the hardest thing she had ever tried to do.

"How could I give lectures?" she asked herself over and over again. "Hardly anybody in the audience could understand what I was saying!"

She knew that her voice was not right and that her speech was blurred and indistinct, even though she and Teacher still worked on it for hours at a time. In fact, it was so bad that some people thought she ought not to try to talk at all. And she knew that, too. Perhaps, if she tried to lecture, her audiences would walk out before she had said more than a few words.

Teacher would have to go on the trip with her, of course. And Helen hated the thought of dragging Teacher away from her husband and the home she loved so much. But Teacher herself made the decision, with her fingers pounding in Helen's hand:

"Come on!" she spelled out one day. "Come on! Let's get started!"

From the very beginning, the lectures went well, although at first Helen was anxious and worried.

It was true that her audiences could not understand her, and Teacher had to repeat nearly everything she said.

But people had heard about Helen Keller ever since she was a little girl. And they wanted to see her. What they saw was a tall, slender young woman, beautifully dressed and attractive. Except that she always seemed to look straight ahead, you'd hardly know that she was blind, they thought.

They marveled at the ease with which she moved about, with Teacher's hand lightly touching her elbow. The rough, tomboy games Teacher had played with Helen when she was a little girl had given her confidence. She did not move timidly, or shuffle along. And her audiences admired her courage in trying to talk, even though it was not easy to understand her.

So began long weeks and months of travel back and forth across the country. Fast trains, slow trains. Timetables, so hard on Teacher's eyes. Strange cities. Strange hotels, where Helen could not find her way around. A different place each night.

And always, wherever they were, Helen was worried about Teacher's eyes. Teacher never complained, but Helen could feel, as they walked about together, with Teacher's hand on her elbow, that Teacher did not move as quickly or as confidently as she had in the past. Sometimes Teacher would hesitate for a long time before they started across a street. One day, in Buffalo, New York, Teacher did not see some steps and fell down them, badly injuring her shoulder.

As soon as Teacher was able to travel after the accident, they returned to Wrentham. They went on no more lecture trips for several months.

But lecturing was a way of earning a living. So they started out again, after Teacher had recovered, and kept on—until one terrible night in Bath, Maine.

Teacher had had a bad cold for days. That night she was so ill that she could hardly drag herself back to the hotel after the lecture.

Helen woke up in the night, worrying about her. When she went to Teacher's bed and took hold of her hand, it was burning hot. And Teacher's fingers did not move in her palm. Teacher's forehead was terribly hot, too. Although Helen could not hear her, she was moaning and out of her head with fever.

All the rest of that night Helen sat by Teacher's bed, unable to help her. It would have been impossible for her to find her way down to the hotel lobby to get help. And she could not have used the telephone even if she could have found it. For nobody could have understood her.

There was nothing she could do but wait. Finally Teacher roused herself enough to reach for the telephone. Then the hotel manager brought a doctor.

After that, Helen and Teacher did not go on any more trips alone.

18.

Narrow Escape

HELEN WAS about to drift off to sleep when she first noticed the smell. It was like the smell of steam coming up in the radiators.

"Funny that the heat should be coming up at this hour of night," she thought.

It was very late, and everyone else in the house was asleep. But going to sleep was not easy for Helen these nights.

Teacher was ill. She was spending the winter in Puerto Rico, where it was warm and she could get plenty of sunshine. While she was away, Helen was back in Alabama, staying with her mother and her sister Mildred, who was now married.

It was the first time Helen and Teacher had been separated for so long since Teacher had come to her when she was a little girl. Helen was very lonely without her.

She worried about Teacher, too, even though Teacher punched out long letters to her in Braille—almost as if she were talking to her.

Turning restlessly, Helen again noticed the smell. It was different now. It smelled as if someone might be burning leaves outdoors. But nobody would be burning leaves late at night.

"Probably they had a bonfire this afternoon," she thought, "and the smell is still in the air."

She turned over once more, in a determined effort to go to sleep. But suddenly she threw back the covers and sat up.

The smell had changed again. It was tar. And burning wood! And it was close by!

For an instant she had to stop and remember which direction to go to her mother's room. She did not know her way around in Mildred's house as she knew the way around her own home in Wrentham.

But in seconds she was at her mother's bedside. She shook her and grabbed her hand.

"Wake up, Mother! Quick! Fire!"

Fortunately Helen had remembered to close her door when she left her room. For when her mother opened it again, the whole room was in flames! The closed door had shut off the draft and kept the fire from spreading out into the hall.

Quickly they roused Mildred and her husband. He called the fire department. Then they got out of the house as fast as they could—which wasn't any too soon. The house was badly damaged before the firemen had the fire under control.

"If we'd got here five minutes later, your whole house would have gone up!" the fire chief told them.

There was something else that frightened Helen, although she did not mention it to anyone. If she had not been able to smell, she would have been burned to death. The fire had started right under her bed!

But what worried her more was that her mother and the others might have been burned to death too. She wrote to Teacher:

"It seems as if I could never sleep quietly here again without putting my face down close to the floor and hunting all over for an odor or a hidden spark."

The long, lonely winter finally ended in April, when Teacher came back from Puerto Rico feeling better. It was a good thing that she was, for she and Helen had a hard job to do.

They went back to Wrentham—not to stay, but to sell their beautiful home that they loved so much. It almost broke their hearts to leave it.

But the house was too big and too expensive to keep up.

Besides, it was usually empty. For John Macy was no longer teaching at Harvard, and the writing he was doing now kept him, too, away from home most of the time.

In Forest Hills, a suburb of New York City, Helen and Teacher found another house. It was an ugly little house, but it was the best they could afford. They made it as attractive as they could.

All this would have been much harder for them if they had not had Polly Thomson to help them. Wonderful Polly Thomson, with her sense of humor and the Scottish burr in her speech!

Helen and Teacher had gone back to Wrentham after that terrible night in Bath, Maine, knowing that they could not go on any more lecture trips alone. They were wondering how they would manage when a friend told them about Polly Thomson.

Polly had come over from her home in Scotland on a visit and was staying with relatives near Boston. As it turned out, her "visit" lasted more than forty years! Polly was young, not long out of school, where she had studied to become a secretary. The friend arranged for her to meet Helen and Teacher.

They liked her immediately, and she liked them, and before long Polly had become a mem-

ber of the family. She had been living with them
when Teacher had become ill, and she had gone
with Teacher to Puerto Rico to take care of her.

The marvelous thing about Polly was that she
seemed able to do almost anything. Helen and
Teacher began to find this out when Polly went
on a lecture trip with them after they had moved
to Forest Hills.

Teacher had always had a hard time reading
railroad timetables. The print was so fine. Even
if she held the timetable right up against the
tip of her nose, she could barely make out the
letters. And she was too proud to ask for help.

"It's so humiliating," she said, "to keep asking people to help me all the time. It makes me
feel like a helpless old woman."

Now that Polly had come, Teacher no longer
had to worry about timetables. Nor about looking up telephone numbers nor finding her way
about in strange cities. With Polly between
them, Helen and Teacher could cross a busy
street quickly and confidently, without worrying about oncoming cars, which Teacher sometimes did not see.

One of the first things Polly did for them was
to straighten out their money affairs, which
were in a terrible mess. From then on, when they
were traveling, Polly handled most of the
money. Teacher's eyesight was so poor that

sometimes when she and Helen were leaving a taxicab she gave the driver a five-dollar bill instead of a one-dollar bill and told him to keep the change. And Helen, of course, could not read the figures on the bills at all.

Polly quickly learned the Manual Alphabet. That was a big help to Teacher, for Polly could read to Helen—especially the mail, which was always heavy.

"She is the most wonderful thing that ever happened to us!" Teacher would often spell into Helen's hand. And Helen always agreed.

During the first few years Polly spent with them, Helen and Teacher were often short of money—even though Helen had swallowed her pride and had written to Andrew Carnegie, accepting the pension he had offered her.

The fees they received for their lectures were not large. And they never seemed able to keep money when they had it. Always people were asking for money to help the blind and the deaf. Helen and Teacher could never refuse them.

If John Macy had lived, he could have helped them. But one day after they moved to Forest Hills, a telegram came for Teacher. John Macy had died, in a strange city, far from home.

Polly was supposed to be their secretary, and when they had a maid she wrote letters for them. But there were many times when they could not afford a maid. Then Polly cooked and scrubbed and washed for them.

Teacher could no longer see well enough to do much work around the house. There were some things Helen could do, like making beds and washing dishes, but she couldn't scrub or wash clothes.

Polly worked for a salary when they could pay her. When they did not have the money to pay her, she worked for nothing, for she loved them.

It was wonderful to have a friend like Polly. It meant a great deal to Helen, for she had a big worry, that she could never put out of her mind.

19.

Behind the Footlights

HELEN'S BIG worry was about Teacher. Over and over again she would say to herself:

"What would become of Teacher if anything should happen to me?"

Again and again through the years the doctors had operated on Teacher's eyes. Each operation had been less successful than the one before. Now the time was coming, Helen thought, when an operation would do no good at all.

So long as Helen lived there would be a little money coming to her—Mr. Carnegie's pension. But if Helen died, that would stop. Then Teacher would be left alone, blind and penniless.

"I *must* find a way to earn enough money so I can put some away in the bank for Teacher," Helen would tell herself desperately.

Finally a way opened up. Helen took it, even though she knew that she would be severely criticized for doing so.

This was in the days before talking movies. In those days people used to go to vaudeville shows. Vaudeville was rather like an indoor circus. It had acrobats, for instance, and sometimes trapeze artists and trained animal acts. In every city there were one or two vaudeville theaters, with a new show every week.

Usually in a vaudeville show there was one act that was called the "headliner." Sometimes it was a famous actor or singer or violinist. Sometimes it was a speaker. These people were very highly paid. The offer Helen received was to be a headliner in vaudeville—for more money than she had ever earned in her life before.

She knew what people would say—that she was showing herself off for money, like a freak in a circus sideshow. But that didn't matter to Helen. The only thing that did matter to her was that she would earn enough money so that she could save some for Teacher.

Someone would have to appear on the stage with her, of course, to repeat to the audience what she had said. Although she and Teacher still worked on it for hours at a time, her voice was not much better, and it was hard for people who did not know her well to understand what she was saying.

"Why don't we let Polly appear on the stage with me?" Helen asked Teacher. "I'm afraid the footlights, which they tell me are very bright, will hurt your eyes."

But Teacher said no. Vigorously and emphatically her fingers spelled into Helen's hand:

"I know you are doing this for me. Don't ever think I'd let you go alone, without me! It's my job to help you, *and I'm going to do it!*"

Polly went with them, but it was Teacher who walked out onto the brilliantly lighted stage night after night, even though the footlights hurt her eyes so that she could hardly bear it. Sometimes she couldn't. Then Polly would take her place.

Helen, Polly, and Teacher were all very uneasy about this new venture. So were the two men who owned the chain of theaters in which they were to appear. One of the partners thought it was a big mistake.

"Look," he said to his partner, "people come to the theater to laugh and have a good time. They won't come to listen to somebody they can't understand and feel sorry for!"

But the other partner would not give up. "Let's try it out," he insisted. "Helen Keller is the most famous woman in the world. I think people will come to our theaters to see her and listen to her.''

They tried out the act in a small theater in Mount Vernon, a suburb of New York.

The curtain rose, showing the stage set like a beautiful living room. At one side was a grand piano, and on it a big vase filled with flowers. Teacher, in a handsome, new formal evening gown, stood in the center of the stage—trying not to blink, although the light hurt her eyes. She made a little speech, telling about the things that Helen Keller could do and how she had learned to do them.

While she was speaking, Helen, with Polly at her side, waited tensely in the wings. She knew her part well, for they had rehearsed it many times. Teacher finished her speech, the orchestra played some music. Then Polly gave Helen a little nudge, and Helen walked out onto the brightly lighted stage.

She reached out, found the piano, and running her hand lightly along the edge to guide herself, walked along until her hand touched the vase. She knew now that she was where she was supposed to be, and she stopped and faced the audience. Then she made a little speech, asking help for other blind people, with Teacher repeating her words after her.

The applause she received as the curtain went

down was warm and enthusiastic. This audience loved her.

"Things went well tonight, but the real test will come at the Palace," the doubting partner said. The Palace, in New York City, was the largest and most important vaudeville theater in the country.

"This was a suburban audience, and they loved her," the partner went on. "But the Palace crowd will be different. They won't be coming to see Helen Keller. They'll be coming to see a good show. And if they don't like it—it will be just too bad for us!"

The Palace was packed the day Helen's act opened there. It always was packed when a new show opened. At first, while Teacher was making her speech, the audience was silent. Some people shifted uneasily in their seats.

But when Helen Keller walked on, beautifully dressed, smiling, keeping time a little to the music as the rhythm came to her through the soles of her feet, the audience broke into admiring applause.

And when Helen, with a happy smile, thanked them, explaining, "I can hear your applause through my feet," the audience went wild. Some people stood up and cheered. There was awe in the theater manager's voice as he said later:

"Miss Keller, you had 'em eating out of your hand."

And so it continued as Helen, Teacher, and Polly traveled about the country for two years with their act. There was hardly a city in the United States where they did not appear. In many of them they were invited to come back. The audiences loved Helen. And Helen loved them.

At the end of her speech the audience was invited to ask questions. Some of the questions they asked were silly and stupid, but they were never cruel. One that was always asked was:

"Do you shut your eyes when you go to sleep?"

Helen would always act as though nobody had ever asked her that question before! She would wait a moment, as if thinking it over. Then she would smile and reply:

"I don't know! I've never stayed awake long enough to find out!"

She enjoyed the trips even though she knew some people thought she ought not to be in vaudeville and were saying unkind things about her. She made friends with everybody—the acrobats, the soft-shoe dancers, the dogs, monkeys, and seals in the trained animal acts.

Although Helen enjoyed the vaudeville tours, she knew they were hard on Teacher. So she was relieved when, at the end of two years, she was able to give them up. She had earned and saved enough money so that she no longer needed to worry about what would become of Teacher if anything should happen to her. And now she had a new job.

Helen had been asked to join the staff of the American Foundation for the Blind, and this was a job she was to hold for many years.

The Foundation does a great many things to help the blind. It works with schools for the blind and helps to train teachers for them. Sometimes it gives scholarships to gifted blind students, to help them finish their education.

The Foundation works with Congress and with the state legislatures to get good laws that will help and protect blind people. Through articles in newspapers and magazines, and by radio and television, it tells seeing people what the blind need and how to help them, and shows businessmen that there are many jobs a blind person can handle just as well as a seeing person can.

Working with the Library of Congress, the Foundation also makes "talking books for the blind." These are phonograph records. Somebody reads a whole book aloud, it is recorded, and a blind person can play the records on his own phonograph!

"I wish I could hear one of those records," Helen told Teacher, when she learned about these "talking books." "This is one of the finest things that has ever been done for the blind."

One of the first books recorded was one Helen herself had written.

To do all these and other things, the Foundation must have money, and Helen's job was to help raise that money. Again, she had to travel. She went to cities and towns all over the country, telling people about the Foundation and asking their help. People listened to her and gave generously.

But now it was Polly who traveled with her. Teacher's health was failing rapidly. She was in pain much of the time. And she was now as blind as she had been when she was a little girl, before the first operation on her eyes.

Teacher wept as she pleaded with her doctor to operate on her eyes just once more. He finally agreed, although he told her he felt sure the operation would not do her any good. And it didn't.

One evening in October, 1936, Teacher felt well enough to sit in a big armchair in her room. Helen and Polly were with her.

Herbert Haas, a young man who worked for them, had been to New York, to see the rodeo, in Madison Square Garden. And Teacher laughed with delight as he tried to imitate the *yippees* of the cowboys.

"I do wish you could hear him, dear," her fingers spelled in Helen's hand. "He is so funny!"

It was a happy evening for Teacher, with people she loved. That night she went to sleep and slipped quietly away into another world— a world where there is no pain nor any illness. And nobody ever goes blind.

20.

The Teacher Book

IT WAS Christmas morning, 1946, when Helen Keller and Polly Thomson walked sadly around a big black hole in the ground where their home had been.

The house, in the country near Westport, Connecticut, had been their home for seven years. And they had loved it as Helen and Teacher had loved their home in Wrentham years ago.

Now it was gone, completely destroyed by fire. Just a hole in the ground, with blackened bricks and pieces of charred wood strewn about and partly burned papers blowing around in the wind.

Helen could not see these things, but she had no need to. For a heavy blanket of smells hung over the place. Not the pleasant smell of a bonfire or logs burning in a fireplace. But the bitter, sickening smell of burned paint and varnish and cloth.

"What about Teacher's Tree?" she asked.

Close by the house had grown a beautiful little oak, which they called "Teacher's Tree" because she would have loved it so.

"It's dreadfully burned on one side," Polly's fingers told her. "But it may not be dead. We'll wait and see when spring comes."

She and Helen had been in Europe when they had heard about the fire. At the end of World War II they had been asked to go over and find out what would be needed to help the thousands of people who had been blinded, in battle and in the air raids. When the bad news reached them, they had hurried home by plane, arriving on Christmas Eve.

Now as they walked about the ruins of their house, Helen kept thinking of other black holes in the ground. Not only in countries they had just visited, but in many other parts of the world. There had been homes there, too, before the bombs came. Thinking about those other black holes in the ground, Helen could not feel sorry for herself.

"We have wonderful friends and enough money to live on, which millions of people do not have," she said.

"Yes," Polly's fingers spelled. "Think of all those poor people where we've been in Europe! They've lost their homes, too. They need our help, and we mustn't let them down!"

Yet the loss of their own home was a staggering blow to both Helen and Polly. There is so much more to a home than just a house.

Helen sighed, thinking about the "Teacher book." This was a book about Teacher, on which she had been working for years. She had wanted to write it because she felt that Teacher deserved a great deal more credit than she had ever been given.

"Wherever Teacher and I went, people always made a fuss over Helen Keller," she had told Polly. "But they seemed to forget that it was Teacher who made it possible for me to do the things I did. The honors should have gone to Teacher, not to me. I want everyone to understand this and to love Teacher as I have loved her."

With this in mind, she had worked on the book. She had finished almost three-quarters of it and had put it carefully away in her desk before she and Polly left for Europe. Now the book was nothing but ashes. And all the letters Teacher had written her in Braille and her own notes in Braille that would have helped her remember things she wanted to put into the book were ashes, too.

"When I think about the Teacher book being burned up, I feel as though someone had cut off my right arm," Helen said sorrowfully as she and Polly returned to the home of some friends where they were staying. "But as soon as I can, I shall start all over again and rewrite the Teacher book."

Many months passed, however, before Helen could start writing another Teacher book. She and Polly had a big job to do, and they had to start at once. That job was to raise money in the United States for millions of people in other parts of the world who were not only blinded by the war, but were left homeless and hungry, too.

Money was needed to buy food and clothing for those people and to build new homes for them. More money was needed to rebuild schools for the blind and to replace the Braille libraries which the bombs had destroyed. In some countries money was needed to replace the Braille printing presses that had been melted down to make ammunition.

Helen and Polly knew a lot about raising money. They had done it for the American Foundation for the Blind.

So they started traveling again, all over the

United States. But this time, in her speeches, Helen tried to make her audiences feel what it was like to be a young, blind soldier who would have to spend the rest of his life in darkness. Or a frightened little blind girl groping her way around in the ruins where her home had been, trying to find her mother whom the bomb had killed.

So earnest was Helen's plea that it was hardly necessary for Polly to repeat what she had said. People understood. And the money poured in.

Yet often, as she and Polly traveled about the country, Helen's thoughts turned to the Teacher book. Finally she started writing it over again in the home of a friend. A new house was being built for Helen and Polly, but it was not finished yet. Helen wrote on a borrowed typewriter since her own had been destroyed in the fire.

She had no notes, none of Teacher's letters, nothing to help her remember things. Just a typewriter and a pile of blank, white sheets of paper.

Hour after hour she sat at the typewriter, living through in her memory the years when Teacher was with her, trying to bring back those years and put them down on paper.

When she finished, it was not the kind of book she had always planned to write. It was much shorter, for one thing. And she had not started out from the beginning and gone right straight through the years as she had in the first book. Instead, she wrote about things as they came back to her in bits, here and there. Little things sometimes—funny and gay. Happy times, at Red Farm and in their home at Wrentham. And some sad times. The years at college, when she was so worried about Teacher's eyes. The pain of knowing that Teacher was going blind.

And all through the book—on every page, in every sentence—Teacher. So clear and warm and alive that when you read the book you can almost see her, gazing lovingly at Helen as she spells words into her hand.

Teacher, who, as Helen wrote, had left "the wonder of language" in her hand.

21.

One Summer Day

HELEN KELLER, returning from an early morning walk, stopped for a moment beside a handsome oak tree near the sunny, pleasant white house that was home to her and Polly Thomson.

The house had been built where the burned house had been, in the country near Westport, Connecticut. There were no traces of the fire any more.

And Teacher's Tree, so badly burned on one side, had not died, but had grown big and strong, with fine branches and beautiful, glossy leaves.

"What a perfect summer morning!" Helen thought, as her hand stroked the bark of the tree. "And how good it is to be home again!"

She and Polly had returned the day before from a trip through Norway, Sweden, and Den-

Laws must be passed, providing adequate pensions and medical care for them. Schools must be built for them, and teachers trained.

Jobs must be found for those who could work. Businessmen must be shown that there were many things a blind person could do as well as one who could see. Organizations like the American Foundation for the Blind were needed to do research and to supply Braille books and magazines, as well as special equipment for the blind. And, of course, money must be raised to help pay the expenses of these organizations.

Since the end of the war, Helen and Polly had been invited to many countries to help plan and carry out this work. They had done everything they possibly could.

Always in Helen's heart was the hope that there would come a day when no blind man anywhere would have to go shuffling along a street with a tin cup in his hand, begging. That had been Teacher's hope, too.

"It's a pretty big hope," Helen said to herself, as she stood in the early morning sunshine, stroking the bark of Teacher's Tree. "But I think we've made some progress."

She thought, however, that she and Polly might not be able to take any more long trips.

"Polly has come home terribly tired," she told herself, "and I am tired too—a little!"

She could smell coffee and toast as she went on into the house. Polly was getting breakfast. Helen went out to the kitchen. Her job was to squeeze the orange juice.

Polly had already cut the oranges in halves and had placed them near the squeezer and the glasses. By the time the orange juice was ready Polly had finished putting things on the breakfast trays. Then she and Helen went upstairs. Each carried her own tray, since Helen had no trouble finding her way about in her own home.

They went to Polly's room, and Polly climbed back into bed with the morning papers, which she read while she drank her coffee. When the coffee was finished she spelled the news to Helen.

The maid, who came to help them during the day, brought in the mail. There were lots of letters. Helen Keller had been one of the most famous people in the world for more than seventy years—ever since she was a little girl. Famous people get a great deal of mail.

Polly read the important letters first, and spelled them to Helen with her fingers. Those that were not so important she laid aside. She would answer these. Helen would answer some of those that were important.

They spent the morning at their typewriters.

Polly's desk was downstairs, in a room off the front hall. Helen had a study upstairs.

Next to her typewriter was her Braille machine, which works somewhat like a typewriter. On this she wrote letters to her blind friends and things which she herself wanted to read over later, such as speeches.

Before lunch Polly came in, and Helen handed her the letters she had written. Polly looked them over carefully. If there was one single mistake in the letter—even the tiniest mistake in typing—Polly would give the letter back to Helen, and Helen would do it over. This was something Teacher had always made Helen do, and she insisted that Polly make her do it, too. But today there were no mistakes. Polly held a heavy piece of cardboard underneath the space where Helen would sign her name, so that her signature would be even, and Helen signed each one.

A guest came for tea that afternoon. After the guest left, Polly cooked dinner. When she and Helen had eaten, they washed the dishes. Polly washed, and Helen dried. Once Helen gleefully handed a plate back to Polly to wash over again. A bit of food was still stuck on it. Polly had not noticed it, but Helen's sensitive fingertips could feel it.

"You r-r-rogue!" Polly said, roughing the

"r" in her Scottish burr. Helen couldn't hear her. But they both laughed.

They spent the evening in their quiet living room, a soft breeze stirring the curtains at the windows and bringing the scent of dew on grass and flowers into the room.

Bedtime came early, for they were both tired. Helen was in bed when Polly came to tuck her in and say good night.

"Now you go to sleep!" Polly said as she leaned over the bed, with Helen's fingers reading her lips. "No magazine tonight!"

A new Braille magazine had arrived that day, and Polly had seen Helen carrying it upstairs with her.

"No, dear—no magazine tonight," Helen said meekly.

Polly turned out the light and left the room. Helen waited a moment—Polly might come back.

She did not reach for the magazine. But from under her bed she brought out her Braille Bible —too big and too thick to be left on her night table. Thoughtfully she turned the pages until she found the one she wanted.

Smiling in the dark, she passed her fingertips lovingly over the worn Braille dots:

"The Lord is my Shepherd . . ."

THE MANUAL ALPHABET

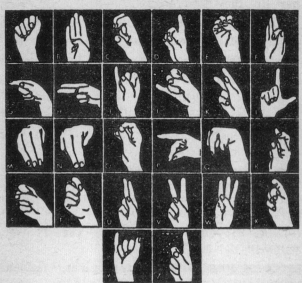

THE BRAILLE ALPHABET

A B C D E F G H I J

K L M N O P Q R S T

U V W X Y Z

159

If you enjoyed this book, you will want to read these other absorbing TEMPO BOOKS.

THE STORY OF FLORENCE NIGHTINGALE by Margaret Leighton. The fascinating, true-life story of the Lady with the Lamp who made nursing a noble profession.   T59   50¢

AMERICA AND ITS PRESIDENTS, by Earl Schenck Miers. Vivid portraits of the thirty-five men who have held the most important job in the world.   T71   50¢

NATIONAL VELVET, by Enid Bagnold. The beloved tale of a girl and her horse.   T5   50¢

REBECCA OF SUNNYBROOK FARM, by Kate Douglas Wiggin. Quaint little Rebecca will capture your heart.   T63   60¢

ANNE OF GREEN GABLES, by Lucy M. Montgomery. Red-headed, dreamy Anne brings happiness, love and laughter into the lives of her foster parents.   T64   60¢

DADDY-LONG-LEGS, by Jean Webster. The appealing, unforgettable story of an orphan and a mysterious millionaire.   T55   60¢

BAMBI, by Felix Salten. The much-loved story of a forest deer.   T51   50¢

ORDER from **TEMPO BOOKS**, 51 Madison Avenue, New York, N.Y. 10010, enclosing check or money order—no currency or C.O.D.'s, please. Please include 10¢ per book for postage and handling. A complete list of titles is available upon request.